Seeking Peace:

My Journey

"Always be ready to make your defense to anyone who demands from you an accounting for the hope that is in you; yet do it with gentleness and reverence."
— I Peter 3:15,16

"And he has committed to us the message of reconciliation."
— II Corinthians 5:19

Seeking Peace:

My Journey

by

Atlee Beechy

Distributed by:

Pinchpenny Press
Goshen College
Goshen, Indiana 46526
Telephone: 219-535-7463
Fax: 219-535-7293

Seniors for Peace
Peace Center
College Mennonite Church
1900 S. Main Street
Goshen, Indiana 46526
Telephone: 219-535-7262

Library of Congress Control Number: 2001087501
Copyright © 2001 by Atlee Beechy

All Rights Reserved

Printed in the United States of America
by Evangel Press, Nappannee, Indiana

Dedication

I dedicate my story to my wife Winifred, active partner in my peace journey for nearly 60 years. Her roles have been many and important—homemaker, mother, grandmother, companion, hostess, and friend. She has been an author, editor, teacher and a member of the Mennonite World Conference Presidium. She has been involved in peace and service. Her discipleship has been marked by deep commitment to Jesus and his ministry of reconciliation. She reached in compassion to the oppressed, wounded and suffering. Her witness against racism, poverty, sexism, materialism, and militarism has been strong. She has stood up for the liberation of all caught in bondage. Without her my peace and justice journey would not have been possible.

Acknowledgements

I acknowledge with gratitude my parents' sowing and nurturing the seeds of peace and justice in my heart. I am grateful for the many lessons that Karen, Judy and Susan—my three daughters—taught me and for their creative help and strong support for this project. Six grandchildren, three sons-in-law and many students, peers and teachers have added important learnings.

I am thankful that God arranged for hundreds of creative and courageous peacemakers to touch my life and keep my inner fires burning. I also owe a large debt to Seniors For Peace Coordinating Committee and my K-group for helpful counsel. Stuart Showalter brought excellent editing and management skills to the project. Hilary Breeze's creative ideas find expression in the lay-out of the manuscript. Edna Kennel, long-time artist friend, created the imaginative sketches and the cover. To all, I again say thank you.

Atlee Beechy, October 2, 2000

Table of Contents

Foreword -- xi
Early Days, 1914-36 --- 1
Inner-City Shock and Challenge, 1937–43 -------------------- 9
Marriage and Family, 1941+ --------------------------------- 15
Civilian Public Service, 1943–46 --------------------------- 23
Post World War II, Europe, 1946–49 ----------------------- 29
Goshen College Years, 1949–83 ---------------------------- 37
India Sabbatical, 1960–61 ---------------------------------- 41
Goshen College in the 1960s ------------------------------- 53
Vietnam War, 1966–74 --------------------------------------- 69
Nigeria–Biafra Visit, 1969 ----------------------------------- 99
China: Educational Exchanges, 1980+ --------------------- 105
China: Teacher Exchanges, 1981+ ------------------------- 125
Retirement, 1983+ -- 131
Ireland, 1985–86 -- 155
Seniors for Peace, 1986+ ----------------------------------- 171
Peacemaking: an Ongoing Response, 1990s ------------- 179
Transitions: Places and People ---------------------------- 189
Visions of the Future, 2000 -------------------------------- 197
Bibliography --- 209

"They shall beat their swords into plowshares, and their spears into puning hooks; nation shall not lift up sword against nation, neither shall they learn war anymore."

—Isaiah 2:4

Foreword

As Atlee Beechy sketches his life story in *Seeking Peace: My Journey*, he invites us to join him in a spiritual pilgrimage—to become peacemakers and disciples of the Prince of Peace. His story begins in 1914 in the first months of the Great War in a Mennonite home in rural Holmes County, Ohio. It leads to the campus of Goshen College and on to teaching in inner-city Columbus, Ohio, followed by Civilian Public Service as a conscientious objector during World War II.

The story unfolds into Atlee Beechy's long life as servant to the world. We see him directing relief and reconstruction work in post-war Europe and continuing to minister in a series of crisis areas: in newly independent India, the civil rights movement in the United States South, the war in Vietnam, civil war in Nigeria, violence-ridden Northern Ireland, communist-occupied Poland, impoverished East Africa, post-Mao China. His peacemaking and justice-seeking journey is projected against the tragic backdrop of the most violent century in all human history.

This story is not a conventional autobiography. *My Journey* is invitational: come, join in the calling to be an agent of reconciliation. Atlee tells his life story modestly, with an air of reflective detachment. He amplifies the lean autobiographical outline with perceptive paragraphs from his journal, a private treasure that has entries dating back to his youth. Included, in addition, are letters speaking truth to entrenched power, thoughtful meditations and, most important, poems in free verse. Atlee has been a closet poet in our midst. I would encourage two readings of this slender volume: first, a fast-paced reading from beginning to end to grasp the broad contours of Atlee's fascinating life; second, a more deliberate-paced reading as a book of meditations, a few pages at a time, pausing often to ponder prayerfully.

The spiritual tone of My Journey may be found in Atlee's journal entry as a 22-year-old in his first week of teaching: *"Bless each girl and boy. . . . O God, soften my heart with the spirit of Jesus. . . . Keep me humble and grant me a sense of quiet confidence. . . ."* The grace of humility, art of blessing, the spirit of Jesus — these are essential ingredients in the peacemaking to which Atlee invites us.

Few Mennonites have traveled this earth more widely than Atlee and Winifred Beechy. Like a seasoned international journalist, he has been fresh on the scene of the world's trouble spots. Particularly captivating are his insights from a sabbatical year in India, where he observes with the perspective of the nonviolent Gandhi a liberated people plunging into the grubby tasks of fabricating a new state. He and Winifred served as a peacemaking presence amidst the shambles of that most tragic of wars: Vietnam. His sensitive ambassadorial skills are revealed in the more extensive section devoted to the establishment of the China Educational Exchange, he being the principal architect of that highly satisfying program.

Atlee's role as a peacemaker is illuminated in his gentle but persistent confrontations with militant adversaries such as Ian Paisley, vitriolic Protestant clergyman in Belfast. Endearing is his caring relationship with an ailing George, his ardent foe on issues of Vietnam. Atlee's journey is sprinkled with poignant moments such as a meeting in a hospital parking lot with his daughters just after he is informed of the gravity of his cancer.

As one reads My Journey, one is drawn to reflect on what are the qualities that shape a person of peace and reconciliation. In Atlee one senses peacemaking is rooted in familial love — affection among husband and wife and children and grandchildren. One sees this life shaped by a Mennonite faith community centered in the Christ of the Cross and the calling to love and do justly. One sees it nurtured in the bonding of a teacher with students. One sees it enriched in a network of friends and small groups of kindred spirit. Critically important have been the gateways to service of the Mennonite Central

Committee and Goshen College. In Atlee's story one becomes profoundly aware that the Lord of his journey and his companion is Christ, the Prince of Peace.

Knowing Atlee as a dear friend and now reading *My Journey*, I sense that he has brought special gifts to the calling of peacemaking. As some peacemakers are gifted in the arts of mediation, others adept in prophetic analysis of the human condition, others agile as disputants in theological and ethical dialogue, others skilled as strategists in orchestrating peaceful change — Atlee brings a special pastoral quality to peacemaking. Like an Old Testament patriarch, he gives blessings wherever he goes. He radiates an invitational spirit: "Come, let us be friends." Enemies become friends. In him peacemaking is carried on the wings of a psalmist, in the ways of an empathetic listener, in the graces of amity and hospitality.

Seeking Peace: My Journey thus should be read as a book of meditations on peacemaking, told in stories and reflections from a journey with one who is among the most beloved of his generation.

Robert Kreider
North Newton, Kansas
September 26, 2000

Early Days, 1914-36

Chapter One

My journey began in the small town of Berlin, Ohio, on October 27, 1914, the year World War I began. Anti-German sentiment was alive. Berlin's best known citizen was Atlee Pomerene, U.S. Senator from Ohio, who was helpful to Amish and Mennonites during the war. In recent years Holmes County's most important exports have been trail bologna and Swiss cheese and its best known imports have been tourists who come to explore Amish country.

There were no options for conscientious objectors in WW I other than being assigned to regular military camps or going into prison or hiding. Those drafted were often harassed and punished for refusing to wear the military uniform and for disobeying orders. Some were sent to federal prisons. Two Hutterite conscientious objectors died in Fort Leavenworth prison in Kansas because of the treatment they received. When the parents came to pick up the bodies of their sons, they found that their sons, who had refused to wear the uniform while living, were in death dressed in uniforms by the authorities. What a travesty! Those who opposed buying war bonds also were harassed. Bishop Samuel Miller of the Mennonite Church in Walnut Creek, Ohio, who also served as editor of the Sugarcreek Budget, the weekly newspaper of the Amish, was hauled into a Cleveland court by a zealous prosecuting attorney for printing a letter from a Kansas reader who objected to buying war bonds. After spending one night in jail and paying a $500 fine, Miller was released. I believe Senator Pomerene may have helped cool the ardor of Cleveland's prosecuting attorney. I began life in a world at war.

Memories of life in the beautiful hills of Holmes County, Ohio, are good. I got an early start in school, entering first grade two months short of my fifth birthday. According to my mother, I pestered her to join my two slightly older best friends in school. Apparently, she cut a deal with the teacher that I could attend school until the weather turned ugly. Fortunately, the weather was good all year! An abandoned poodle left in our barn and a brown and white Shetland pony (not abandoned) were important in my growing up years. When my brothers or friends were not available to play catch with me, my blacksmith father used his "strong and sinewy hands" to play, even on Sundays. I was attracted early to Christ's teaching and example of loving the poor and the oppressed. I felt an awakening desire for God's grace but I do not remember the exact time I came to faith. Love nudged me in my faith experience rather than fear of hell fire.

Developing Faith and Peace Concerns

I owe a great debt to my parents for starting me on my service and peace journey. I was my mother's errand boy in her outreach to the elderly, the sick, widows, widowers and those with other needs. My parents introduced me to Jesus and his compassionate responses to pain and suffering of his day. The biblical teachings about peace were discussed at home and in Sunday school. When I was 10 years old, we visited the Ohio State Penitentiary and an area devastated by floods, and I began to be aware of human pain and need. In parenting, my mother and father modeled peace and service living. Sports and two close elementary school friends taught me some practical lessons in getting along. My two older brothers, Orin and Ralph, were helpful mentors to me as I was growing up. Later, they became strong supportive counselors as I accepted calls to overseas relief and peace service and to join the Goshen College faculty.

Visiting relief workers and missionaries often stayed in our home. They brought exciting shafts of light and opened windows to needs in the larger world. When I was 13, I was baptized into the Martin's Creek Mennonite Church. Love and laughter were not so much talked about, but were actively present in our family relations. Church, school, service and work were important to my parents. At age 14 I became part of the neighborhood threshing community along with our team of horses. This experience was an important step in moving me toward maturity.

In my teen years a lively Sunday school teacher, David Mast Jr., had the audacity to ask what Jesus had to do with how I played basketball, handled money, took care of animals and treated my school friends. In high school, an articulate teacher and coach, Milton Smith, sharpened my appetite for current events and history. He also emphasized respect for the body, good sportsmanship and teamwork in playing basketball. During my Goshen College years (1931-35), classes, student activities and professors Guy Hershberger, Harold Bender, Edward Yoder, Olive Wyse, Mary Royer, John Umble, Sanford Yoder, Willard Smith and others opened the window to my rich Anabaptist peace heritage. For two weeks in 1935 I taught summer Bible school in the Mennonite mission in Chicago, another important growth experience for me. A loving family, the model of others who lived the Jesus way of compassion, my beginning awareness of the needy, and the violent nature of our world were determinative factors in my faith development.

My journey has been challenged by questions. What is the nature of God's reconciling purposes and actions in the world? How do I maintain hope in the midst of violence, suffering and despair? In what do I invest my life? How do I respond to the needs and problems of the human family? How do I express my faith and peace convictions? What is the heart of my faith?

Looking for God?

I find God in star-filled heavens,
       in majestic catherals,
       in bamboo churches,
       in simple houses of worship
       wherever God's people live
       and love and serve the world
I find God everywhere:
       in children's laughter and singing birds,
       in red roses, heavy with dew and fragrance,
       in the seasons' changing colors,
       in the touch of a loved one's hand,
       in the breaking smile of a suffering friend,
       in the road less traveled,
       in the weathered face of a 90-year-old,
       in the bonding of family and community,
       in the words and spirit of a friend in prison,
       in literature, music, art, humor and games
       in sharing bread, pain, joy and hope,
       in forgiveness and reconciliation after tears,
       in worship, prayers, silences, hymns and the Word,
       in students' reaching, struggling, connecting, finding,
       in the mystery and wonder of creating and discovering,
       in the faces and courage of refugees and war sufferers,
       in the beauty and promise of an expanding sunrise,
       in unrationed, amazing grace that forgives and renews and
       in the faces of those who work for peace and justice.
       Thank you God for all the ways You come to me !

What Faith Means to Me

Faith is to be lived. The Beatitudes describe what being Christian means. Jesus calls me to discipleship in Matthew 5. Paul's words in I Corinthians 13 remind me "that now these three remain: faith, hope and love. But the greatest of these is love." Paul's words in II Corinthians 5: 18-19 call me into Christ's ministry of reconciliation. Certain faith beliefs are guiding my peacemaking journey. God is a God of love, desiring peace and justice for all. God is the God of the universe and also the God of the individual and the community. Jesus is Savior, Prince of Peace, and Mediator, and through His death and resurrection I am reconciled to God. Jesus shows me God's loving and just nature and is my example. I am saved by accepting God's costly, reconciling grace. Grace continually comforts, confronts, heals, forgives and transforms. Grace frees me from undue guilt and fear and liberates me for witnessing to and caring for the world. Grace is God's wondrous gift! Unrationed grace leads me into discipleship and keeps discipleship from becoming rigid and an end in itself. Grace deepens and broadens my conversion. That process never ends!

God's grace is indeed Good News. I respond to God's grace by loving family, neighbor, stranger and enemy. My vocation is to live and teach Christ's love way morning, noon and night. Peacemaking is always within the context of justice-seeking. Grace and peacemakers help transform enemies into friends. I try to respond to hostility in the spirit of Jesus with a heart full of grace. To me peacemaking is central, not peripheral to my faith, to be pursued as long as God's gift of life comes to me.

Peace begins in the heart and embraces all of life. Peace is a gift of God's grace and a state of quiet confidence and security. Peacemaking involves biblical study and much prayer. Peacemaking is being God's reconciling, transforming presence and action in all relationships and situations. Peacemakers search for people caught in suffering, hate, fear, oppression and

violence. They live the nonviolent Jesus way of active witnessing to individuals and structures that create and perpetuate injustices and violence. They invest their lives in building Shalom communities, toward the goal of the well-being of all people.

For me, there are seven dimensions of peacemaking:
- Helping people to be reconciled to God, themselves and to each other;
- Breaking down walls that discriminate and divide;
- Affirming good and protesting evil;
- Reducing violence, injustice and war and their causes;
- Providing conflict prevention and mediation education;
- Building peace-generating individuals, congregations and communities;
- Increasing love and expanding interpersonal and inter group reconciliation in the family, congregation, school, community, nation and world.

My vocation is outlined in Isaiah 61:1-2 and is restated by Jesus in the announcement of his ministry in Luke 4:18-19:

> *The spirit of the Lord God is upon me, because the Lord has anointed me to bring good tidings to the afflicted: He has sent me to bind up the brokenhearted, to proclaim liberty to the captives, and the opening of the prison to those who are bound; to proclaim the year of the Lord's favor and the day of vengeance of our God; to comfort all who mourn.*

Inner-City Shock and Challenge, 1937-43

Chapter Two

Despite my intentions, I feel my words are somewhat idealistic and pious. I turn to the real world and confess some troubling questions and experiences I have faced in my peace journey. My first real testing came in my six years of inner-city teaching.

In 1937, Wilbur W. Miller, assistant superintendent of the Columbus, Ohio, public schools, invited me to teach in a large, inner-city elementary school. Moving from a one-room school of 58 students in the peaceable kingdom of Holmes County, Ohio, into the inner city brought culture shock, more than I later felt in many of my overseas assignments! I discovered a new world of personal and structural violence, poverty, prejudice, pain, greed, hate and struggle.

My school principal used an unusual way to measure the school's effectiveness. He kept count of the number of windows broken in the school annually. He believed the lower the number broken the more effective was the school's program. He theorized further that the quality of the formal and informal athletic programs strongly influenced the frustration and satisfaction level of students and their window-breaking behavior. I had primary responsibility for this area of activity at the school and enjoyed the challenge. With time, I became more troubled as I began to sense the complexity of inner-city problems. My concerns about racism, economic injustices, poverty, Mennonite affluence, piety, peace and nonviolence increased.

The following selective journal entries written during the first two months of the 1937-38 school year reflect my emotional state and spiritual dependency on God as I began my teaching in the inner city.

September 10, 1937

God, help me deal with the problems I face today. Bless each girl and boy. I again dedicate my life to you, O God. Soften my heart with the spirit of Jesus. May your love become my compelling inspiration in the days to come. Keep me humble and grant me a sense of quiet confidence. Amen and good night.

September 14, 1937

Classes went fine today, but the playground with 350 girls and boys running around in a space 80 by 100 yards presents a real challenge. There were many fights. "He called my mother a name" seems to be an acceptable excuse for a fight. May God grant me continued inspiration and patience for this demanding work.

September 30, 1937

God, I have been seeing so much evil, so much suffering and violence that sometimes I wonder if it's worth trying to do anything here. But then your spirit comes and nudges me to stay at it. Thanks.

October 17, 1937

I was home over the weekend and there found again quietness and freedom from the cares and problems of the inner city. It would be easy to become satisfied in such surroundings away from all the pain and poverty. And yet I can't feel comfortable doing that. Deep down I thank you, God, for this opportunity of learning and serving in this place. God, I need you more than ever before. God, grant me wisdom, patience and courage for each day.

November 27, 1937

I was a little late in arriving at the Martin's Creek church this morning. The main part of the church was filled. I sat in the anteroom where I could still see the preacher and he could see me. During the announcements he said, "This afternoon at two o'clock (I felt his eyes fall on me) will be the funeral of Atlee Beechy." There was shocked stillness followed by a correction from Preacher Simon Sommers. It was strange to hear your own funeral announced from the pulpit! I recovered. It reminded me that some day the announcement will come. The minister was very apologetic.

Later Reflections

I was the sole male teacher. Most days I was the playground game organizer, policeman, referee, conflict mediator, and sometimes judge. One day I was urgently called to the playground area where several hundred yelling students were gathered around two seventh-grade boys who were fighting. One had a knife and was obviously trying to use it. The danger to the other student was real. There was no time for a consultation on nonviolence. My call for a halt was ignored. At an appropriate moment I grabbed and twisted the arm of the student with the knife, and in my most authoritative voice said, "Drop it." Fortunately, he did. The exchange moved to the office. No, this experience is not a model for peacemaker intervention. But how does a nonviolent peacemaker respond to such conflicts? How does a loving God relate to the violence in the inner city?

Dealing with many situations of this kind forced me to think about the biblical meaning of love, nonviolence and

A Prayer

God, increase my love power.
God, transform my thoughts, ideas,
Emotions, words and deeds into
Building Shalom.
Amen.

justice. I began to move from seeing nonresistance primarily as non-participation in war to thinking of it as an active, reconciling spiritual and social power that transforms people and situations. Such a concept opened the door to more options. Getting rid of knives, crack houses, guns, land mines and bombs is an important element in peacemaking. But equally or more important are conflict prevention, mediation, reconciliation and building community.

Another persistent question followed me—why were some students able to break out of prisons of violence, poverty and racism and others not? The six years of inner-city teaching were packed with many questions and learnings. I learned much about myself, human behavior, structural violence, faith, prayer, conflict and God's concern for the inner-city world. My students taught me much about courage, toughness, hope, love, trust and gentleness. Early Saturday morning breakfasts with groups of my students along the Olentangy River remain highlights in my memory bank. I began to be aware of the sins of prejudice and racism and the need for Christ's reconciling work in my heart. I highly recommend inner-city teaching as a valid service vocation. It also is excellent preparation for peacemaking in our violent world.

Marriage and Family, 1941+

Chapter Three

Winifred and I grew up in quite traditional families in which church and worship were important and in which family relations were somewhat paternalistic. Work, caring for the sick and elderly, moral behavior and following church teachings were emphasized. Participation in sports and drama were frowned on by a few in my congregation, but my parents took an enlightened view, not only permitting but encouraging my participation. Social dancing was out of bounds, but folk games were tolerated. We knew our parents loved us, though verbal expression of such feelings was not very frequent.

Winifred and I first met during the 1938 Fourth of July weekend at Goshen College. My brother came to Goshen to visit his girl friend, and I tagged along. He and his friend suggested I find a date and join them in their activities. I confess to feeling anxious as I ventured into the "yes and no room" in Kulp Hall and waited as the matron called Winifred. My research had indicated that she was attractive, intelligent, friendly, had a mind of her own, was active in religious life, and possessed a good sense of humor.

The two dates we had that weekend confirmed the validity of my research and lit the love fire. It took some time, energy, and long-distance courting from Columbus, Ohio, to Sterling, Ohio, for the fire to burst into full flame. We discovered a growing number of shared interests and also some differences. Falling in love was exciting and a little scary. In time, our relationship moved toward marriage. The decision as to when to get married was complicated by several factors—the war clouds of World War II, the uncertainty about the draft, and the fact that I had two older brothers who had not yet taken the marriage leap. Should I show them the way? Yes! We decided to get married in the spring of 1941.

When a teacher friend of Winifred heard us talking about wanting to make our marriage special, she offered wise counsel. "Why don't you write down your marriage expectations. I will be glad to be witness to your statement." We followed her unconventional advice.

Our Marriage Expectations

1. We will not let anyone, or anything, alienate our affection for each other.

2. We will not let the "sun go down on our wrath" and will settle our differences before we sleep.

3. The decisions about car, money, and other possessions will be jointly made.

4. We will keep alive the small courtesies toward each other. We will not let them fall by the wayside.

5. We will bring our peeves and grudges into the open.

6. We will keep outside interests alive, maintain friendships, and participate in worthwhile projects.

7. We will not take each other for granted and we will not be afraid to let the other person know that love is much alive.

8. We will have a "date" each week and an occasional dinner date as the budget allows.

9. Criticisms and adjustments will be made charitably and intelligently.

Spring 1941   Signed: Winifred Nelson
                        Atlee Beechy
               Witness: Jean Mayberry

These words pointed a direction, described an early pattern of relationships, and reflected our deep love and commitment to each other. It has served us well over the past 59 years of partnership. The memo was lost for some years, but was found in a perfectly logical spot, our wedding scrapbook. Since then it has provided a model for others and been part of the wedding service for others. Most recently, we stood up with our granddaughter Katie and her husband during their wedding. We shared our Marriage Expectations, and they followed with their own, comparable list of goals.

Our wedding was simple and lovely. It took place in the old Goshen College Assembly Hall, where we had gathered for daily chapel during our student days. The date was May 24, 1941. S.C. Yoder, President of Goshen College during our student days and a beautiful, spirit-filled person, tied the knot. As was the custom at that time, each of us repeated phrases of the vows as the minister addressed them to us. I forgot to repeat one phrase, the promise to support Winifred through "prosperity," although I did promise to support her through "adversity." Instead of stumbling back over the omission, I decided to go on. Winifred noticed! Often she reminds me of my slip and of her lifetime efforts to see that we "do not become prosperous." We have not done so, except in terms of family and friendships. Next to our faith decisions, the decision about life-partnering was, for us, the most important. The journey has been interesting, joyful, challenging and deeply rewarding.

Our marriage has been greatly enriched by three wonderful daughters. Karen was born September 10, 1944, in Gerber Memorial Hospital in Fremont, Michigan. She came while Winifred and I were serving in Civilian Public Service. Judy was born on May 6, 1948, in Basel, Switzerland, while we were in MCC European relief service. Susan joined us on November 3, 1949, in Goshen, Indiana, the first year of our tenure at Goshen College. During the first 15 years of our married life we lived in 21 different places. This moving suggests a degree of mobility, mostly related to service and education assignments. We cherish those years, for they were rich in relationships and in spiritual and human experiences.

Shortly after coming to Goshen in 1949, we purchased two lots on Woodward Place for $1,200. In 1956, Salem Bank and the Beechys launched a faith venture, cooperating in building a house that Winifred designed, and that house became our beloved home for the next 40 years. Winifred was a little concerned that building a house might tie us down too much, but that did not happen. We enjoyed sharing our home with friends and acquaintances from all over the world. A tradition, which became a highlight for family and friends, was the annual New Year's Breakfast, which featured homemade breads. When we were on sabbaticals or service assignments, our house was occupied by seminary students, missionaries on furlough, former MCC workers, or faculty colleagues.

Our family expanded through the addition of three quality sons-in-law: Gerald Kreider, Gordon Dyck, and John Enz. Our daughters and their husbands continue to invest their lives in human services—four in teaching and two in social work. Their marriages led to another quality infusion into the family, the coming of six wonderful grandchildren, Katie and Emily Kreider, Teresa and Jeffrey Dyck, and Alice and Nicholas Enz. The grandchildren are a great joy and have taught us much about life, relationships, love, hope, gifts, and learning.

Selected Family Vignettes

> *Winifred, the children (who were six, eight, and eleven), and I were eating lunch in the Ohio State Union Cafeteria in the summer of 1956. After a bit, I noticed an older, rather distinguished looking man watching the activity at our table. When he got up to leave, he came to our table and said to me, "You may not know it, or believe it, but you are a millionaire with this beautiful family." I thanked him, and the children giggled their thanks. Later, they wondered if they couldn't cash in some of the million dollars he said they were worth!*

Judy, at age five, joined her parents one summer in doing some MCC-related service for several weeks. Her first words on arriving back in our Goshen College Coffman Hall apartment were, "I am so glad to be back home. This is where I belong."

During Easter weekend, in 1991, our children surprised us with an early 50th wedding anniversary celebration in the Pocono Mountains in eastern Pennsylvania. They got us to Akron with the collaboration of John A. Lapp, who invited us to Akron for a "made up" MCC assignment. Upon arrival at the place of celebration, the children ushered us into the prepared bridal suite where we found Winifred's wedding dress and a dress suit for me for the replaying of our wedding reception.

The weekend exchanges, and the shared memories, renewed our hearts. A second aspect of the celebration that continues to feed our souls are the 150 letters from dear friends who answered the children's invitation to share thoughts and greetings on this occasion. What a priceless gift!

Letter from 16-year-old Granddaughter Katie, April 1993 (written from Kodaicanal, India, during her parents' sabbatical assignment)

"John and Dorothy Nyce received a pack of The Goshen College Records the other day and allowed us to read through them. I came across an eye-catching article, "Beechys Link Peace with Faith." To tell you the truth, nothing in the article struck me as being new; after all, I've heard the stories of travels, journeys, and various other feats that the elder Beechys have accomplished in the name of love and peace. However, Grandma's quote had an impact on me. "People reach that age and feel that there is no more they can do, so they go off to Florida and play shuffleboard, but they should be encouraged to realize that they still have resources." . . . I realize how lucky I am because I have two very unique, interesting, inspiring (& I could go on) people that I can call my grandparents. They know what the real important things

> in life are–knowledge of the world around us and family–as opposed to praising material possessions. My grandparents are out fighting for peace and a better world. Granted, I may be partial to my own grandparents, but I really am proud to be a part of this family and thank God every day for my luck. I am especially proud to have you both as grandparents (if you still haven't figured that out by now)."

Response from Winifred to Granddaughter Katie, May 1993

> "Your letter of April 15 arrived several days ago and made that day a red-letter day, to say the least! It is quite humbling to receive so much praise. We can't tell you how much we appreciate your opening your feelings and thoughts to us! . . . Actually, I do not see our lives as especially heroic. We have tried to use what God-given abilities or aspirations we have for the benefit of others less fortunate as a matter of everyday living, nothing spectacular. But, anyway, thanks for seeing us as special, even though we may not be able to live up to it."

The shadow of cancer has had a significant impact on our family. Youngest daughter Susan's diagnosis of breast cancer in 1984 was followed by a mastectomy, radiation and chemotherapy. Eight years later a second mastectomy followed, with a repeat of radiation and chemotherapy. In 1997 she had to undergo additional treatment for another malignant tumor. Her strong spirit and positive attitude have been important weapons in her fight against this dreaded disease. She has been an inspiration to many. Winifred had ovarian cancer surgery in 1989, followed by a single radiation treatment. Oldest daughter Karen was diagnosed with breast cancer in 1998 and underwent a bilateral mastectomy. We are grateful that, at this time, all three are in remission.

In February 2000 I became the fourth member of our family of five to be invaded by cancer. Currently, I am being treated for an unusual form of skin cancer. God's unrationed grace and the strong support of family and many friends have been comforting realities during the darker hours.

While Winifred was waiting to go into surgery at the

Indiana University Medical Center in Indianapolis on May 24, 1989, our 48th wedding anniversary, I wrote her a love letter. I concluded with these words,

> *"I could go on and on, but on this special day I list several reasons in support for my case that I love you with my total being! We do not know what the next hours will bring, but we know that our love remains indestructible. Thanks again for who you are and for your contribution to me, our family, and a host of others scattered across the world. The day will bring changes, which we need to face, but let us draw from a rich storehouse of wonderful memories and continue to live in hope."*

Words on the Altar in the Indiana University Medical Center Chapel

> *"The eternal God is our refuge, and underneath are the everlasting arms."*

Upon Reaching 85 Years of Age

> *On October 27, 1999, I reached the milestone of 85. The weekend before, grandchildren Teresa and Jeff Dyck and Jeff's wife Lara were visiting our daughter Judy and her husband Gordon. Winnie and I were invited for a "small" pre-birthday party. When we arrived, we were greeted by over 75 friends and relatives who had gathered to celebrate. Our daughters and their families from Pennsylvania and New Jersey surprised us! Winnie turned 85 in February, 2000. For this special celebration our children had a wonderful family gathering at Pokagon State Park during Easter weekend. God's grace blessed, enriched and bonded these gatherings.*

There is mystery, wonder and joy when God's amazing grace ignites love, and love penetrates human relationships–family, marriage, neighbors, strangers, aliens, refugees, and enemies.

Civilian Public Service, 1943-46

Chapter Four

I introduce this section with the words shared by an important U.S. Selective Service official during his 1945 visit to Hill City, South Dakota, Civilian Public Service Camp:

This whole business of war is all wrong. War never settles anything, never will. It is tragic that all men are not doing something constructive like you are. In normal times the people are all for you. Now you are not so popular but keep it up and they will appreciate you again. Psychologically, I don't like the word objector. It denotes you are against something. You are against war but you also are for something; you are for peace. That should be emphasized.

Registration for the draft in 1941 and induction in October, 1943, into Civilian Public Service, the U.S. government-approved alternative to military service, raised other questions in my peace journey. What happens to a historic peace church when the nation goes to war? What is the essence of the Mennonite peace witness? How important is the peace witness to the preservation of religious freedom and to the church's life and witness?

In my CPS assignment as educational director, I was responsible for organizing educational, recreational and religious activities for more than 100 men in a base camp at Sideling Hill, Pennsylvania. The so-called "work of national importance" was conservation. In October, 1944, I became director of the base camp at Hill City, South Dakota, where the work project was building a large, useful dam. In January, 1946, I was transferred to Akron, Pennsylvania, where I coordinated material aid collections and shipping for the Mennonite Central Committee relief program. I was discharged from CPS in May but continued in the material aid assignment until November, 1946.

Women played an important role in CPS. They contributed much through their service as dietitians, nurses and matrons in base camps. In addition, these women had a positive, humanizing influence on the men. Some wives and women friends provided important spiritual and emotional support by living and working near the camps and units. Others helped keep hope alive through visits and thousands of letters. Winifred served as dietitian at Sideling Hill and as matron in Hill City. In between she took time out to give birth to our first daughter Karen.

Women also made a very significant peace witness through COGS (Conscientious Objector Girls Service). Women volunteered to work in mental hospital units where CPS men were serving. They strengthened the concept of voluntary service. Their presence improved morale. They also made a significant contribution by helping to reform mental health care in the hospitals by their quality service and witness. Rachel Waltner Goossen tells this important story in the book, *Women Against The Good War*, 1997.

My CPS experiences were important in shaping my peace convictions. God used CPS to deepen my faith and to discover the Mennonite family-its diversity, commonality and its strength and weakness in peace witnessing. My peace agenda continued to expand during this period to include life style, environment and many forms of injustices and human rights violations, including racism and sexism. My identity as a peacemaker was strengthened by being part of a clear witness against war and a participant in the larger peace movement.

I was impressed, but sometimes troubled a little, by the witness of my fellow campers. I also was challenged by the courageous witness of many men. The diversity in the camps caused some tensions which both tested and enriched us. Radical Love, a follower of Father Divine from New York City, bunked along side Amish and Mennonite campers. A Jewish lawyer and a professor of sociology brought new insights into the discussions of the peace witness. The death of a camper while operating a large tractor brought pain and grief to the camp but also spiritual growth. I learned much about human nature, frustration, faith expressions, tolerance and intolerance, and the power of hope and community.

The dropping of the first atomic bomb on Hiroshima on August 6, 1945, came as a great bewildering shock. Only dimly did I see the implications of this horrifying act at the time.

A Related Journal Entry, August 6, 1993

> *Today, on the anniversary of the dropping of the first atom bomb, I heard a reporter interview the bombardier who released the bomb that killed over 120,000 women, men and children in Hiroshima. The reporter asked, "Do you have any second thoughts on the part you played in this terrible tragedy? "Oh no," he quickly replied, "I simply followed orders." And then he added, "If I had been an infantryman I could not have raised my gun, aimed and killed a Japanese." And yet the act of releasing the bomb that killed thousands, most innocent civilians, didn't seem to trouble his conscience. What twisted ethical and moral confusion war brings!*

In spite of some weaknesses, I believe Civilian Public Service contributed significantly to a broadened world view and to spiritual growth of most participants. In a February 13, 1996, letter a participant reflected on his experience in these words:

> *One of the highlights of my life were the days I spent at Hill City CPS camp. I value highly the experience I had there. Fifty years later finds us transferred from being the young men of yesterday to being the grandpas of today. The question is, How well have we succeeded in passing on our rich (peace) heritage to this generation?*

A commonly heard evaluation by CPS men was, "I wouldn't take a million dollars for the experience but I wouldn't give a nickel for another one."

CPS contributed significantly to the various Mennonite groups by building a strengthened Mennonite identity and by increasing mission, service and peace awareness. CPS accelerated inter-Mennonite exchange and cooperation, generated leadership for the church and community, and was a critical factor in bringing about much needed reform in mental hospital care and treatment. CPS tested the peace convictions of participants and the church's commitment to this witness. Finally, Civilian Public Service was an important witness to the larger church and to the world regarding conscience, freedom of religious expression and the biblical concept of peace. Howard Schomer, a widely known United Church of Christ leader, participated in CPS in the 1940s. In a CPS evaluation conference in 1991 Schomer reflected on his experience. He said,

> *You Mennonites are the recognized and seasoned veterans of Protestant Christian peace-seekers in this war-addicted world. You have much to teach churches like mine that have only recently been trying to become nonviolent citizens of this planet. . . . I now hope that the transfusion which the Historic Peace Churches have given the whole ecumenical fellowship means that Mennonites will not be lonely in their (peacemaking) efforts. Even Congregationalism, in its new life in the United Church of Christ, will surely lend a hand.*

Civilian Public Service was an improvement over the way conscientious objectors were treated in World War I. The CPS experience helped bring about the I-W arrangement under U.S. Selective Service. Conscientious objectors throughout the 1950s had greater service options. For me CPS was an important growth experience that broadened and deepened my peace convictions. In November, 1946, largely because of this experience, Winifred and I entered MCC relief service in Europe for two and a half years.

Fifty years ago CPS tested peace convictions of 5,000 Mennonite men and the church's commitment and support of our Anabaptist peace heritage. Where are we today? How are we responding to the unprecedented peacemaking needs and opportunities before us? Are peace and justice central or peripheral to our faith? For me they are central. If Mennonites are to be spiritually healthy, effective witnesses, and have integrity in our peace and justice witnessing, I believe we need first to face and deal with the violence in our own hearts and actions. Such an approach calls for transformation of persons, relationships and structures. God's unrationed, reconciling grace is the only power that can cleanse, transform and renew our hearts. If we open ourselves fully to God's grace, our peace and justice witness will burn with new brightness. James Brenneman has it right when he writes that "Jesus, the peacemaker, far from being a liability to outreach, is instead the most important asset we have in our witness."

Post World War II, Europe, 1946-49

Chapter Five

"War is all hell."   -General William T. Sherman, Civil War

I faced another set of questions as I became involved in overseas relief efforts and peace and justice work. How do I maintain sanity and compassion when responding to the suffering war brings? How do I respond to the religious, political and ethical issues that war and peacemaking create? How does the church maintain a clear peace witness in the midst of nationalism, political and ethnic pressures? How does the church "engage the powers" and work toward reducing and eliminating the causes of war and violence?

Orie O. Miller, long-time executive secretary of the Mennonite Central Committee, often used the words of Jesus from Matthew 13:38, "the field is the world," to enlarge the vision of MCC workers. He opened my door to an expanding MCC overseas ministry to war sufferers and peacemaking and invited my participation, first at Akron and then in Europe. Miller had the gift of placing challenges in front of young people and inviting them to respond. His expression of confidence in the person was in itself an important factor in developing leadership. I marvel at the risk Miller was willing to take by giving former CPS men (including me) heavy relief and refugee assignments, far beyond what our educational and vocational preparation and experience should have allowed us to undertake.

Here, after a brief summary of my reflections of post-war conditions, I share selected journal entries in the hope they will help readers understand something of the nature of MCC relief efforts in Europe and the impact of these experiences on my peace and justice journey.

From November 1946 to March 1949 I served as MCC European area director, working out of headquarters in Basel, Switzerland. Winifred managed the headquarters and was the hostess of the center. The MCC family grew to well over 100 committed North American workers along with many Europeans who played important roles in the program. All gave themselves freely in a compassionate ministry to war sufferers. They inspired and enriched me.

General William T. Sherman knew what he was talking about when he said, "War is hell." World War II cost an estimated 20 million military and civilian deaths. New technologies of killing (culminating in the development and use of two atomic bombs), military occupation of many areas, and "saturation bombing" of cities, particularly in Germany and Japan, contributed to making this war the costliest in history. United States defense expenditures for the war, 1942 through 1945, totaled $3.11 billion dollars. The bombings left few buildings standing and created an indescribable wasteland of rubble. The economic, cultural, emotional and spiritual destruction and dislocation were massive.

Images of the war remain in my mind even after 50 years. I still see the endless lines of refugees coming from the east with few or no possessions but with amazing spirit and hope. In memory, I see emaciated faces of the returning prisoners of war and the indescribable horror images of death in the concentration camps. At one time MCC was providing 80,000 meals a day. I remember feeding kitchens and the malnourished children and elderly coming for bread and soup. I recall despair and apathy but also much gratitude in their faces and voices. To rebuild self-respect and social fabric MCC workers established community centers where people could work on a variety of self-help projects.

Mennonite Central Committee responded to the emotional and spiritual scars of war in other ways. One effective channel was through international work camps with participants from countries that had been enemies in the war. One Dutch participant told how he struggled with his memories of the German occupation at the beginning of the camp. His feelings of hatred gradually dissolved and at the end he said, "I now know these Germans as personal friends." A German pastor commented, "The distance for the Dutch to come to reconciliation is longer than for the Americans."

After the war North American Mennonite colleges provided scholarships to European students. In one sense the college campuses became places of reconciliation. Swiss Mennonites hosted German children for brief recovery periods and contributed food to MCC feeding centers in Germany. MCC was involved in bringing French and German Mennonite pastors together in the spring of 1948. At the beginning the emotional climate was tense but through worship and sharing the walls began to lower. Tears flowed indiscriminately as pastors found each other again. Harold S. Bender and C.F. Klassen took leadership in planning discussions and conferences on the biblical basis for peace-related topics. Discussions with the Dutch Mennonite peace group took place. Connections were re-established with leaders of the various Mennonite groups. Re-building relationships between European and North American Mennonites in the post-war period was important.

November 13, 1946

> *Today I got my first taste of being involved in relief work. I helped to distribute food and clothing in Arnhem. I wondered what was in the hearts of the people who came to receive from our abundance. Three young Mennonite women, refugees who had lost their families and all their possessions coming out of Russia, helped in the distribution. En route back to Amsterdam they sang hymns. My inner tears flowed as they sang, "Great Is Thy Faithfulness." I tried to imagine what they had suffered.*

February 1, 1947

> The January 31 exodus of 1200 Mennonite refugees from Berlin through the Russian zone was truly a miracle! At the last moment the Russians agreed to let them pass. The prayers of thousands were answered. Our hearts were thrilled and our faith strengthened through this amazing event. We still need to learn how to trust and to use the wondrous power of prayer available to us. In the face of the impossible, Brother C.F. Klassen always said, "Gott kann." He was right again! Klassen gave himself totally to this ministry. Robert Kreider, Peter and Elfrieda Dyck, C.J. Dyck and others also played important roles in this dramatic event. Thank you, God, for answering the prayers of thousands!

August 29, 1947

> The community response to the Walcheren (The Netherlands) builder's unit project is strong. Mrs. Fisher, on learning that the unit would be leaving, said with deep emotion, "When you leave, I'll need seven hankies. This is no funny matter. If it hadn't been for you, we still would not be in our house. . . . You are going to Germany. I guess those poor people have no hope for a better day, but we at least are having our hope realized." The men are making a difference. They are not only repairing houses but are helping to change the climate between the Dutch and the Germans.

September 25, 1947

> Pforzheim is indeed a devastated city! Here on the night of February 23, 1945, over 22,000 people lost their lives in a single 20-minute air raid. In this raid 80 percent of all buildings were destroyed. Today 900 families still live in basements or in garden tool sheds.

October 20, 1947

The terrible destruction of war hit me again as we drove through the city of Hamburg. I thought I was pretty well hardened, but the images I saw today really touched me. I hope I never get "adjusted" to what war does! I noticed a cross still standing on a partially destroyed steeple, an old couple cleaning bricks with a chisel and hammer–a small pile beside them cleaned and millions around them waiting to be cleaned, two young men pulling steel rods from the debris, three children playing house in the rubble and wash hanging on an improvised line between two piles of stones. In addition to the killing and maiming, this is what "saturation bombing" does! The task of physical rebuilding is enormous. But I wonder if the moral, spiritual and cultural rebuilding is not more complex, difficult and important. No one can comprehend all that is involved. There is agreement that the physical needs this coming winter will be very great.

April 8, 1948

Karen seems to have special respect for two MCC workers, H.S. Bender and C. F. Klassen. She always uses Brother Bender or Brother Klassen when addressing them. The rest of the large MCC family are called by their first names. Karen's special respect was tested this evening when she noticed that Bender started eating his dessert as soon as it was served to him. Karen, uninhibited and unafraid as three and a half-year olds are, called down the long table, "Brother Bender, we wait until everyone is served before eating our dessert." Winifred's face reflected a mixture of surprise and shock as probably mine did too. Before we could say anything Brother Bender replied, "You are so right, Karen. I'm sorry, and I thank you for reminding me." It was good to see this human side of Harold. I wish more people could see this side of him.

April 20, 1948

En route to Amsterdam Orie O. Miller talked about his philosophy of personnel, including volunteers and regular employees. He believes the following factors are central: describe the service assignment or job importance in terms of faith and human need; make the person feel needed, wanted and appreciated; and provide reasonable financial security. Orie is a good organizer and planner. He entrusts young people with heavy responsibilities and lets them move ahead. He is knowledgeable in the Bible and in world events. He is an interesting and stimulating travel companion.

April 24, 1948

Gronau is a busy and important place. Much processing of Russian refugees takes place here. Seven hundred refugees are patiently waiting for their ship to be repaired. For them it has been a long and difficult journey. Their faith remains strong, a guiding light in this uncertain hour. The Janzens are giving good leadership here.

May 8, 1948

This past week has been an important one. Judith Ann came to live with us early morning on May 6. I was in CPS when Karen was born. Once again I was absent for this important event. I carefully planned my schedule so that I would be in Basel before the due date, but Judith decided to come early. I thank God that Mother and Daughter are doing fine. Our Swiss Dr. Meyer and the Sisters at the hospital gave excellent medical and personal care. The headquarters team welcomed Judith and are helping in the care of this newest member of the MCC family. Before leaving Akron I remember Brother Orie O. giving his blessing to our having a second child.

September 10, 1948

> This evening I passed through customs at Wissembourg, France. The French custom official asked the routine questions. Where from? Where to? He then asked about my profession. I tried to explain I was a relief and service worker. He interrupted and asked, "Are you Mennonite?" Upon confirmation he wrote on his official form that my profession was Mennonite. Interesting!

October 14, 1948

> I spent several hours with students last evening at Kropsberg, an 11th-century castle in the Palatinate. Twenty Protestant and Catholic students from the University of Mainz had been together for a month with several MCC workers. This was the concluding session. They had been working, playing, discussing, recuperating and sharing their personal and spiritual journeys. They were generous in their expression of appreciation. One needs to cut away some of this as cultural expression but underneath I sensed significant growth had taken place. This, too, is part of MCC's ministry.

May 22, 1948, Letter to MCC Headquarters

> In recent years such terms as Voluntary Service, Refugee Service, and Relief have crept into our vocabularies. These have tended to make us more service conscious. Basically, it seems to me the motivations and pattern in each of these types of service is about the same and should spring basically from inner conviction and concern, rather than only stimulation from outer circumstances. Service seeks and finds opportunities for expression in the situation in which individuals find themselves. Service is the business of every Christian. Service finds its reward in the peace and satisfaction it gives to one who renders the service. Service is a two-way street.
>
> . . . In view of conditions as they appear to us in Europe at this time and out of our own limited experience, we believe that anyone coming

to render any type of service would find it helpful to possess:

An empathetic understanding of the culture and life patterns of Europe, an ability to listen well and a sincere love and concern for the people we relate to.

A sense of stewardship of time, material goods entrusted to us, the power of prayer and most important the Spirit of Jesus whose servant we are.

A sense of perspective on the relationship of one's own contribution to the work of the team, to the work of the Mennonite Church, the larger Christian body and of the importance of opening oneself for learning from every experience.

A sensitiveness to suffering and need which goes beyond sentimentality and goes into action with compassion, seeking to eradicate some of the basic causes of war, suffering and need.

An appreciation and understanding of our rich Mennonite peace heritage and of its meaning for the day in which we live.

A full devotion to the Kingdom of Christ and to his ministry of reconciliation with a willingness to joyfully give oneself to making the service and witness most effective.

My European post-war experience bonded me into lifelong friendships and made a very important contribution to my understanding of the nature and costs of war, significantly deepened my passion against war and greatly strengthened my peace convictions. I was changed by this experience.

Goshen College Years, 1949-83

Chapter Six

The college setting offered new opportunities and questions for my vocation of peacemaking. How does a historic peace church college awaken interest in and concern for the exploding violence in society and world? How does our spiritual heritage inform our response to the needs of the world and our peace and justice teaching and learning efforts? Goshen College administrators made possible my continuing involvement in human rights, relief, development and peacemaking with the Mennonite Central Committee, Church World Service and other organizations during my 34 years of Goshen College service. They also encouraged me to bring peace and justice issues not only into the co-curricular arena but into the curriculum and classroom. I believe this openness helped the college implement its educational goals. My peace and service assignments were personally rewarding, contributed to my effectiveness as teacher and counselor and had value for Goshen College and the Church.

In April 1949 Winifred, daughters Karen and Judy and I moved from Basel, Switzerland, to Goshen College. Susan, our third daughter, was born in Goshen on November 3, 1949. She rounded out my educational and spiritual brain trust! The European assignment involved planning, administering, cross-cultural communication, mediating, counseling and pastoring–good preparation for my educational assignment at Goshen College. During the next 34-plus years I served for periods of time as student personnel dean, director of research, and coordinator of counseling. During these years I always taught at least one course each term. I enjoyed the classroom and found it stimulating and rewarding. I was a full-time teacher of psychology and peace studies the last decade of my Goshen tenure.

Another door opener was Ohio State University's able and frank Professor Ward Reeder, adviser for my master's degree. One day he awakened me to the idea of further graduate studies with these words, "Atlee, it is time for you to get off your fanny and start working on a Ph.D." This wake-up call was important. My graduate studies in personality and counseling psychology introduced me to the complexity, weaknesses and the glory of human personality.

In one sense the period following World War II was a period of transition. Underneath the surface, however, the liberation and civil rights movements were working for change across the world in economic, political, educational, religious, racial and gender areas. Students often participated, and at times held important leadership roles, in these movements. The liberation movements generated tensions and conflicts because tradition, power and change were centrally involved. A growing number of international students, World War II veterans, Civilian Public Service men and returned relief and service workers and missionaries on campus moved Goshen College toward greater international awareness.

As I became more aware of the nature and goals of liberation and civil rights movements, I began to view them as part of my broadening peace and justice agenda and as important for Goshen College. I believe the church's mission is to witness to and care for God's world and to build the new community. At best, Goshen College is both servant and constructive critic of the church. A basic objective of Goshen College is to help the church discharge its reconciling ministry in the world. This involves defining the meaning of faith and mission, critiquing societal and world trends and educating students in the skills and understandings needed to become effective ministers of reconciliation in whatever they do. This includes preparing students for their roles in building peace and justice-minded families, congregations and communities. In the first decade at Goshen College my energy flowed largely into Goshen College's internationalizing efforts and into building a Christian and professional personnel philosophy and program.

India Sabbatical, 1960-61

Chapter Seven

"Love is a rare herb that makes a friend even of a sworn enemy and this herb grows out of nonviolence.... Nonviolence succeeds only when we have a real living faith in God."
  –Mohandas K. Gandhi

My first sabbatical leave from Goshen College was important for a number of reasons. This experience was my door-opener to the history and culture of Asia where almost 60 percent of the world's population live. My knowledge of Eastern civilizations and of their role in world affairs was limited, and my world view was Western and narrow. I discovered that to begin to know and understand the rich, ancient culture of India would require a life-time of study and reflection. My 1960-61 Fulbright lectureship at Allahabad University provided an introduction to Indian life and culture.

I taught undergraduate and graduate courses in guidance and counseling in the Department of Education. I also gave lectures at a number of other Indian universities and study centers. Indian students taught me much about their frustrations, dreams, achievements and problems and about Indian life and culture. My family responded affirmatively to Indian philosopher Tagore's invitation, *"Come inside India.... See it with your own eyes, understand it, think over it, turn your face toward it, and become one with it."* We opened ourselves to the richness of this ancient culture, to its political and economic achievements and to its pain and struggle. It was for us a heart- and mind-stretching experience. We were forever changed by the experience.

I was particularly interested in India's successful struggle for independence from Britain and in Mohandas K. Gandhi's use of nonviolence in achieving this goal. This small, powerful man was key in forcing the British government to grant independence to India in 1947. To me, this revolution was the greatest example in history of the use of nonviolence in bringing about social and political change. How did this happen? What ignited the fire and kept it burning?

Gandhi found inspiration and support for nonviolence in sacred Hindu writings and in the works of Tolstoy. "*My creed,*" said Gandhi, "*is service of God and therefore of humanity.*" He also drew from the life and teachings of Jesus. He said of Jesus, "*The only people on earth who do not see Christ and his teachings as nonviolent are Christians.*" On the role of the teacher, he commented, "*I have always felt that the true textbook for the pupil is the teacher. I have always given first place to the culture of the heart.*" Gandhi advises the peacemaker in these words, "*Be kind, be truthful and be fearless. . . . Do not fear. He who fears, hates; he who hates, kills. Break your sword and throw it away and fear will not touch you.*"

I like Gandhi's words on the power of nonviolence and love:

> *In nonviolence the masses have a weapon which enables a child, a woman, or even a decrepit old man to resist the mightiest government successfully. If your spirit is strong, mere lack of physical strength ceases to be a handicap. . . . All I claim is that every experiment of mine has deepened my faith in nonviolence as the greatest force at the disposal of mankind. . . . The force of love is the same as the force of the soul or of truth. . . . The universe would disappear without the existence of that force of love.*

My sabbatical planted Gandhi's life and peace teachings more deeply into my heart and strengthened my convictions that nonviolence is not only central in my faith but is a powerful tool for bringing about political and social change. The year opened my eyes to the richness of Indian civilization and to India's crucial importance in the family of nations. I also became aware of the United States' slowness in understanding, respecting, and accepting India and its people. U.S. policies often reflected considerable ignorance and limited empathy for India's problems. I discovered that the Indian church, though a very small minority, had an impact on the life of India's education, health care and morality far beyond the size of its numbers.

August 14, 1960

> *India means people, 400 million people (in 1998 over 900 million) living in an area less than half the size of the U.S. One hundred forty million speak Hindi. In addition, India has 13 other major languages and 190 dialects. The population is exploding, even though family planning programs are being introduced. India is a land of great contrasts–wide gaps in wealth and poverty, in urban and village cultures and in regional customs and religions. Caste, though illegal, still has a strong impact on the social structure and behavior of the people. A professor friend from the university was surprised when I thanked one of our employees. He added he feels "thankful too" but would not express it because the person might misunderstand the gesture and take advantage of him.*
>
> *India is currently engaged in a great economic, social and political struggle. She is emerging from centuries of foreign domination. She wants to be accepted into the family of nations. Her people want a better economic life. India is the world's largest democracy. Can India move rapidly enough in finding solutions to her problems so that her people remain committed to democratic principles and peaceful change? The answer is important not only for India but for Asia and for the entire world. The U.S. is slow to see and acknowledge this important fact.*

September 30, 1960

> Dr. Adaval, head of the Education Department, gave an interesting analysis of the national character of India today. After indicating some of the difficulties of making such an analysis, he said that in his mind the real, historic India can be characterized by: 1) Philosophical commitment to idealism–belief in the eternal values of truth, goodness, beauty and the reality of God. 2) An attitude of spiritualism–to emancipate the soul from the body is the highest good, physical comfort is secondary and the soul more important than the body. Both outside and inside forces are helping to break down India's basic values, generating something of a crisis. Many Indians are not aware that this is happening. Adaval believes the old values should not be thrown out and that India should be very selective as to how and what it integrates into its basic philosophy.

November 21, 1960

> Student "indiscipline" is a problem in some Indian universities. Last year an incident involving a student, a theater owner and the police led to a violent confrontation and the closing of Allahabad University for six weeks. Earlier this year there were rumors of a possible student strike. What is the significance of student unrest here, in the U.S. and in many other places? Does this represent commitment to great causes or rebellion against the chaotic world students have inherited? Are students asking for a more personalized and meaning-centered education? Professor Singh and others have been telling me what is wrong with Indian education. They list too much emphasis on memorization and passing end-examinations, irrelevant curriculum content, impersonal and authoritarian faculty-student relations and too few personnel support structures. There is a familiar note in this assessment. Yesterday's newspaper reported that two students had committed suicide because of fear of failure in up-coming university exams.

February 15, 1961

Who can understand India? India is a thousand voices interpreting India's pain, soul and hopes. A root unity sometimes seems totally submerged in the tumult of the shouting over language, geography, politics, education, jobs, economics, religion, power, ethnicity and freedom. Yet underneath runs a strong belief in India's unity and destiny. Should not the U.S. and other developed countries give substantial assistance to India at this time? Helping India to make it would be in the U.S. and world's interest. A remarkable revolution is going on in this place.

March 10, 1961

India continues to strive for truth, beauty and goodness. Sometimes this search gets ensnared in tradition so that India's perspective looks primarily to the past. The West, on the other hand, may have forgotten too well the relevancy of truth, beauty and goodness in its mad rush for efficiency, security and scientific progress. Perhaps the most urgently needed dialogue today is between the idealists of the East and the pragmatists of the West. Each has a great deal to say to and learn from the other. The danger lies in each speaking with rigidity and arrogance before listening and understanding the other. A true spirit of exchange includes mutual respect and caring on both sides. Nations have egos and they swing their political and military weight in support of their own self-interests. Face-saving is important here. Washington seems to have little understanding and appreciation for Nehru's non-alignment efforts.

April 3, 1961

The past, however glorious, cannot alone give vitality and motivation to a people in the present. All the advances in modern science cannot adequately speak to the human soul. There is neither virtue nor vice in traveling by ox cart or jet plane. I hear much talk here about a new synthesis that integrates truth, beauty, goodness, science and technology to serve the human community. The Vice President of India today is the county's leading philosopher. In two years he becomes the President of India. We met him at a reception for Fulbright lecturers. He is personable, articulate and friendly. Maybe we should elect a philosopher as president of the U.S. next time.

April 27, 1961

The departure day has come. A number of people stopped to say goodbye. It isn't easy to leave friends we likely will never see again and a place which has been a wonderful home for nine months. We left Holland Hall by rickshaw a little after 2:30 p.m. and arrived at the station shortly after three. The temperature was hot, around 106 degrees, but this didn't keep 25 friends from coming to see us off. We are leaving something of ourselves and we are taking something of great value from our friends. As the train started moving and after the waving hands dropped from sight, we became a very quiet bunch, each lost in thought.

Postscript to India, the 1970s

I visited India four times for short-term Mennonite Central Committee and Fulbright personnel assignments during the 1970s. The following observations and entries on peace and justice issues come primarily out of a 1972 four-month assignment as interim MCC director in India, but also are partially rooted in our 1960-61 sabbatical year. The 1972 assignment began shortly after the Pakistan/East Bengal war, sometimes called the Rape of Bangladesh. At that time Calcutta was the support base for relief work in Bangladesh. MCC became involved in India famine relief in 1943. From 1943 until the present MCC has worked cooperatively with Indian Mennonites and other social service agencies in important relief and development efforts that today include support for Mother Teresa's work.

May 26, 1972

Today we had an interesting exchange with personnel at the Gandhi Peace Foundation in New Delhi. Radhakrishna, the secretary of the foundation, got together six of his staff. We discussed mutual concerns and peace ideas for two hours. The foundation carries on programs of study and research, education, publications and work camp projects. They focus on emerging tension spots within India. Forty-four field workers implement Gandhian nonviolent methods in field situations. One staff member works with universities in developing peace study programs and with inter-religious groups in promoting peace. Another works on disarmament, and a third is in charge of their excellent library. They have living quarters for up to 30 guests. Students and professors come to spend varying periods of time at the foundation. Special lecturers and seminars are scheduled throughout the year. The foundation is beginning a program in which American students and faculty spend from three to nine months in study here, including some village living experience. They would welcome Goshen College's participation. I believe this could be a very good experience for selected students.

May 27, 1972

Yesterday I spent three hours in the Gandhi Foundation Library reading books on Bangladesh. I was impressed with The Genesis of Bangladesh *by Chowdhury. This is a well documented review of Pakistan history and examines the independence movement launched by East Bengal. The failure of the international community to respond to its moral responsibilities is documented. The U.S. is indicted on this count. Indians can't understand U.S. arms shipment to Pakistan and our failure to protest their use in the genocide of Bangladesh. The Nixon administration lost credibility and is disliked by many here. The India/Russia cooperation pact of August 1971 came in part because of U.S. actions against India. The mood today is markedly different from 11 years ago. On one hand there is disappointment, hurt and anger toward the U.S. At the same time India seems to reflect a new self-confidence, in part coming out of India's response to the Bangladesh/Pakistan problem.*

June 1, 1972

Today's meeting with Charu Choudhry, 70-year-old Gandhian worker, may well be the highlight of our India stay this time. We spent two hours with this sensitive, compassionate and alert peacemaker. He joined Gandhi's movement in 1925. Years later he and Gandhi traveled by foot through what was then East Pakistan. Gandhi suggested Choudhry stay there and start working at reconciling nonviolently the different ethnic and religious groups in the area. Choudhry organized basic schools and community development projects. Others joined the movement. The government remained suspicious of Choudhry's efforts and took his passport from him 16 years ago. Nine years ago (1963) he was arrested and placed in a Dacca prison. There he continued his peacemaking mission, changing the prison into an ashram.

He was released from prison a few months before we met him at the Gandhi Peace Foundation in Delhi. What an indestructible soul energized this peacemaker! I asked him how he described his approach to building peace? His quick, compassionate reply was, "You must live with the people; you must love them; you must have knowledge of their knowledge; you must plan with them, not for them; you must begin with what they have; and with what they want to do!" What wise guidelines for all development and justice work! Many of his co-workers were killed in the terrible massacres of the Pakistan/Bangladesh War. But he kept hope alive and at 70 is eager to begin his peacemaking again.

June 5, 1972, Dacca

We spent time with Mr. Malcar from the Bangladesh Christian Council. He appreciates Mennonite workers who are serving here. He and others indicate there continue to be serious food shortages with the price of rice reaching a new high. Other problems include transportation of food where it is most needed, gangs and growing lawlessness, natural disasters, water control, housing, unemployment, the economy, and agricultural production. Bishop Blair, a 40-year veteran of the area, confirmed these needs. He remembers Mennonite workers from the 1943 Bengal famine period. He updated me on the religious scene. He is cautiously hopeful about the future.

July 15, 1972, Calcutta

Last evening Winifred and I visited an orphanage and a school for poor children here. Both are coordinated by a 77-year-old dynamo, an early Gandhian peacemaker who is still going strong. She is anti-corruption, anti-poverty, anti-evil and pro-human. She has been in and out of prison and goes her way in spite of many obstacles. The orphanage has 52 boys, ages 5 to 14, and is run on a shoestring by three full-time and some part-time volunteers in an old building in the southern part of the city. The nearby school for children has 92 enrolled and is operated by volunteers. We were impressed by the compassionate spirit of the staff. There is hope when in the midst of the darkness one finds these islands of light and healing.

July 22, 1972, Calcutta

What is my typical day like here? Today's schedule was— 6:15 a.m. wake up call, 7:00 breakfast, 7:30 scanned newspaper, 8:00 left for office, 8:20 staff devotions, visited two MCC food warehouses, reviewed Assam flood relief project, dictated letters, met with Church of God pastor (wants more relief supplies), discussed staff problems, withdrew money from the bank (a major undertaking), lunch, studied hospital ground lease questions, conferred with Mr. Choudhry about Janzen's visas, exchanged ideas with staff about poultry project, and chatted with 63-year-old Major Gardner who was in military service for 37 years and for the past 16 years was Salvation Army canteen director for "down and outers." He is possessed by a wonderful spirit. Love and concern flow freely. I saw his beat-up jeep. He said he wore out many jeeps during his years in military service and now is the time for him to rescue and build up human beings, not wear out jeeps. Returned home at 5:30 p.m.

August 5, 1972, Letter to Prime Minister Indira Gandhi

Congratulations and good wishes to you and your people on this special Independence Day, this day of remembrance, celebration and commitment. Your vision, idealism and courage are a source of inspiration for millions of people all over the world.

I am an American deeply troubled by my country's policy toward India, Bangladesh and Pakistan. During 1960-61 my wife, three daughters and I spent an unforgettable year in Allahabad where I was a Fulbright exchange professor at the University. We discovered during that year something of the mystery, glory, achievements and struggles of India. It was the year of Kennedy's election. There was hope that a new day in India-U.S. relations was dawning, bringing together our common struggles, ideals and hopes. Your esteemed father called for unity within the country, for reduction of East-West tensions and for understanding of India's non-alignment policy. What has happened in the intervening 11 years? My heart cries with inward tears as I sense the growing gulf that has developed. Kennedy's untimely death and the destructive shift in U.S. policy took us down another road.

These past three months here in India have confirmed my earlier observations. The U.S. government fails to fully understand and appreciate India's rich culture, its historic and contemporary significance for world peace, its heroic struggles and its complex problems. My government has assumed it could either force or buy the support of your government. The U.S. decision to give military aid to Pakistan well into the tragic Bangladesh war was both a political and human tragedy and the height of moral irresponsibility. Our limited and tardy response to the massive refugee situation reflected *insensitivity to the human aspects of the situation. I believe the U.S. has been too defensive to India's criticism of U.S./Indo-China policy. I and many other Americans would like to see a sharp reversal of policy direction.*

We wish for you the needed wisdom and strength for the heavy duties history has placed upon you.

*Respectfully yours,
Atlee Beechy*

I received a courteous response from the Prime Minister.

October 12, 1972, Letter to U.S. Senator Edward Kennedy

Among the many strained international relationships facing the United States government none, it seems to me, is more crucial at this time than our deteriorating relationship with India. I spent from early May to mid-August 1972 in India and Bangladesh. This was my fourth visit to this area since spending the 1960-61 school year in India as a Fulbright exchange professor.

My thesis is that U.S./India developments, a growing chain of misunderstanding and bitterness, is crucially related to the possibilities of stability and peace in South Asia and the world. I believe that, in our constant preoccupation with international status and saving face, we are pursuing a relatively sure path of losing face, of rapidly becoming the most disliked nation in the West. I review the reasons for this unfortunate development and suggest some needed directional changes in the enclosed paper. In view of your responsibilities I thought you would be interested.

*Respectfully yours,
Atlee Beechy*

October 19, 1972, Letter from Senator Kennedy

> Many thanks for forwarding a copy of your fine essay on "A Face Worth Saving: India and the Changing Image of the U.S. in the Subcontinent." I was pleased to have an opportunity to look at it before the heavy campaigning began this week.
>
> As you know I could not agree more with your view as to the proper direction of American policy towards the nations of the Indian subcontinent. Our so-called "tilt" last year, and our government's insensitivity to the forces of self-determination at work in East Bengal, simply defied understanding. Again, thank you for writing, and best wishes.
>
> Sincerely yours,
> Senator Edward Kennedy

My 1960-61 sabbatical and my subsequent MCC India involvements have been interesting and instructive. National egos and international relations have an impact on regional and world peace. Socialization for war and violence, hanging on to memories which are cemented into society with ethnic and religious intolerance, slowness to forgive, and injustices and unmet human needs generate violence and war.

The Indian poet-philosopher Tagore speaks to the heart of the larger problem in these words: "East is East and West is West, God forbid that it should be otherwise, but the twain must meet in amity, peace, and mutual understanding . . . [in] holy wedlock before the common altar of humanity."

The search for greater justice through nonviolent means is the world's number one challenge. India, I believe, continues to be an important key to peace in Asia and the world. A brief visit in 1993 reinforced my concerns for India/U.S. relations. Let the U.S. wake up, listen, learn and respond with understanding and assistance to India and the Eastern world.

Goshen College in the 1960s

Chapter Eight

The 1960s were interesting, sometimes frustrating and often conflictive. At times North American campuses were places of creative tension and productivity, and in other periods they were places of turmoil and destruction. Liberation and civil rights movements and world events had an impact on student minds and behaviors. Students reacted against authority, the Vietnam war, and civil rights violations and worked for change in college curriculum and administrative structures. The status quo did not bend easily. Some of my colleagues saw positive learnings taking place in spite of or because of tensions while others wished for a return to less disruptive times. A full audit of those years has not yet been made.

During the 1960s I listened to the personal problems, concerns and struggles of students, including dimensions of rebellion and alienation. I also listened to their dreams, achievements, hopes and commitments. I heard a mixture of mental, emotional and spiritual states. I sensed brilliance and stupidity, idealism and escapism, hatred and compassion, gentleness and frustration, irresponsibility and commitment. It was a time of rationalizing and moralizing, of laughter and weeping, of significant learnings and of idle and serious talk of relevancy. Robert Frost's words shed some light on the student mood of that period:

> We make ourselves a place apart, behind the words that tease and flout. But oh, the agitated heart, till someone finds us really out.

Disabled

The sign "disabled vehicle ahead"
    alerts me to your condition.
    Only momentarily do I think of helping you.
    The turnpike "helpers" will be coming soon.
Sometimes I see students flash their "disabled" sign
    to alert me to their condition.
    "Sorry, I've got appointments to keep,
    lectures to prepare and classes to meet,"
    I explain, and hurry on.
The signs are flashing everywhere
    disabled children, parents, teachers,
    administrators, families, communities,
    congregations, systems, workers,
    relationships and nations.
    I slow down, think about the Good Samaritan
    and return to full speed.
    In the middle of the night I wake and. . . .

Behind the confusion and the searching were questions of personal and group identity, self-esteem, authority, freedom, meaning, faith, relationships, sexuality, vocation and life purpose.

Student Voices from the 1960s:

> "I can't understand why I get so depressed. Why did I do that stupid thing? I didn't want to get involved; why did I let myself get talked into it? What am I really like inside? I'm scared to look. Could anyone love me if they knew?"

> "My father was a pastor but he couldn't help me with my problem. They should have had courses for parents on how to love their children. If someone would have told my mother to show a bit of affection or attention to me every once in a while, I'm sure a lot of my brattiness would have been solved. And I was a brat."

> "How can I ever trust anyone again? I've been let down and hard! I followed him and did everything he wanted me to do. I thought it was for real. I staked my future on him. He promised–but now it's gone, smashed. I don't think I'll ever trust a guy again."

> "I started sleeping with fellows who I didn't even like. I thought I was liberated and could handle it, but I felt rotten, disgusted, guilty, used and angry with myself."

> "My mind spirals back to how hopelessly stupid and full of hate I am. I would often like to apologize for my pettiness, but I can't. The thousands of images and thoughts that flood my mind tire me and I seek for the will to conquer my complexity. I try to give but I have nothing. I try to say 'hope' but I do not hope. I only endure."

A student came to my office in the mid-1960s. His face and body language reflected anger, confusion and despair. Without any preliminaries he blurted out, "I am sick and tired

Who am I?

Who am I?
I have two hands, two eyes, a mouth, tendons and toes.
I eat in the cafeteria, sleep in a bunk bed,
play tennis, go to class, and tell stories.
Who am I?
I sometimes laugh and smile and act sophisticated,
and sometimes glare because of the mess outside
and the turmoil inside.
I hope, dream, love, hate, think, pray.
I want to be loved and accepted.
I want to be an individual and stand on my own feet.
I want to be unique and yet linked together;
alone, but wishing to be bound to others.
And so I am part individual and part other,
vaguely aware of sometimes wanting to be both
at the same time.
Who am I?
The complexity and the task frighten me.
I am confused and afraid.
I talk of this to my friends and I ask them to help me.
I wait for someone to "explain me."
But my friends are trying to find their selves too.
Who am I?
I ask God and search within myself and others.
I search for clues as to who I am.
I don't fully know.
But I can't wait forever.
It's time I get moving,
for if I wait until I fully know,
the game will be over.

-1964

of all the religious double-talk around here. I don't want any of your pious words. All I want from you is a straight answer as to what you believe about God and Jesus!" I prayed as I shared my faith and empathy for his pain and search.

Jesus, in announcing his vocation in Luke 4:18-19, quotes the prophet Isaiah on injustices, liberation and human need. His words have a familiar ring to needs today. Jesus invites his followers to get involved in his reconciling ministry. The late Paulos Mar Gregorios (Paul Verghese), a 1952 Goshen College graduate and Metropolitan of New Delhi, saw the liberation movements as important church agenda for moving toward greater peace and justice. In his book, *Freedom And Authority*, Gregorios writes, *"The women's liberation movement holds within it the germs of perhaps the most significant psychic revolution in the history of mankind."* I agree with this statement. Yes, we are on the liberation road but still have a long way to go in creating a kinder and more egalitarian way of relating between the sexes and the races.

Accepting, respecting, challenging, encouraging, loving and sometimes confronting students are important ingredients in an effective teaching/learning climate in the classroom. They also are important for developing a growth climate in all aspects of college life, including student activities and housing where important learnings take place. Teaching and counseling are first cousins. I view counseling as individualized learning–helping students understand and reduce their inner civil wars, discover and develop healthy personal and group identities and relationships and find faith meanings that lead to commitment to a reconciling life cause. The nature and quality of faculty-student relationships is the key factor in learning and teaching. Teachers, counselors and student development personnel are peacemakers and justice-seekers.

A Prayer at the Close of the Semester

God, we thank you
> For the hours we have been together,
> For ideas, questions, incomplete answers,
> For sharp interactions and strengthening affirmations,
> For enlarging our experience of being and becoming,
> For extending knowledge and deepening emotions,
> For disturbing us through the world's pain,
> For stirring up compassion and the gifts within us,
> For inviting us into your continuing creation activity.

God, forgive us
> For skipping over ideas and issues too lightly,
> For manipulating and stereotyping each other,
> For rationalizing and theorizing too much,
> For judging others and ourselves too quickly and too harshly,
> For being too defensive about our actions and inactions,
> For violating each other's space and personhood,
> For preoccupation with our own needs and wants and
> For ignoring the pain of fellow travelers.

God, grant us
> Connectedness to You and Your purposes,
> Sensitivity to Your Spirit's work in others and ourselves,
> Inner healing woven into indestructible hope,
> Vision of what we may become through You,
> Courage to act in love and to seek justice in the world's classroom
> And much joy and humor for our reconciling journeys.

Excerpts from "Reflections of A Recycled Counselor," presented at the Association of Mennonite Psychologists, 1994

As a counselor who joyously and gratefully lives in God's grace, I believe the spiritual dimensions are important, central for achieving wholeness and for releasing mental and emotional gifts for development and use.

God's Spirit works in human interaction to reveal needs, contradictions, guilt, anxiety and hurts. It also moves persons toward healing, joy and health, gives new meaning to life and provides important resources for meeting new demands. The Spirit moves in powerful and mysterious ways, freeing individuals and then binding them into a new community. There also is a spirit of evil that is real and powerful. The struggle between good and evil takes place in the world and within our hearts. The Christian counselor recognizes this continuing warfare within and in the larger arena. Persons completely dominated by guilt, hate and anxiety are under the power of destructive spirits. The counselor assists counselees in finding release from these through discovering new insights and in the generating power of love, trust, and hope through faith. In the act of faith the individual joins a supporting fellowship of caring and concerned persons. These relationships help the individual establish and strengthen personal and spiritual identity. The individual contributes to and takes from such a community. "God cares," is a powerful sustaining force for the troubled and searching individual. The Christian, however, is not promised a life free from difficulties but rather is assured of resources to live responsibly and joyously in the midst of them. Counselors and counselees who accept voluntarily Christ's invitation are eligible to draw on these amazing resources.

I believe counseling is important, exciting, demanding and challenging. At times it is also frustrating and humbling. Jesus came to set the captives free, to release them from fear, guilt and hate, and to bring fullness of joy and meaning. Christian counselors are instruments through which the troubled and others are helped to find their way to this new and fuller life, and as this occurs, counselors themselves move into new dimension of growth and wholeness.

On The Lighter Side

Sometimes ironic surprises come to peacemakers–and psychologists. In 1977, during a visit to the island of Mindinao in the Philippines, I was introduced to the leader of the National Peoples Army, a revolutionary group fighting for greater independence for Muslims. When he learned that I was a psychologist, his face lit up and he said, "Please come with me to the hills for several days and talk to my officers about psychological warfare. I need your help." From his perspective the request was understandable, but it did catch me off guard. I managed to say that I was sympathetic to his goals, but as a pacifist psychologist I could not use military means to achieve them. I asked if he had heard of Gandhi and how he led the people of India to independence from the British through using active nonviolent weapons. He expressed interest but time did not permit further exploration.

Civil Rights, 1964

I first met Martin Luther King Jr. during his March 1960 visit to Goshen College. I remember a small informal luncheon when Guy Hershberger and King connected in friendly and productive exchange. That evening King spoke to a large college and community audience. I was deeply moved by King's eloquent words. I was challenged to get more deeply involved in the civil rights struggle.

I followed King's courageous witness road with growing interest. I read his articles and books. King was an important influence in my joining hundreds of college and university students, professors and pastors from the North in "the long hot summer of 1964" to learn about racism in Mississippi and to register African-Americans to vote. I saw King's nonviolent message inspire and sustain this diverse group in amazing ways.

Ten Unforgettable Days in Mississippi, August 1964

I arrived in Jackson, Mississippi, August 5, 1964, the day the bodies of Schwerner, Goodman and Chaney, the three slain civil rights workers, were found. Tension, hate and fear dominated the press, the air waves and the informal talk. My 10 days in that climate opened my eyes and heart to the sins of racism and discrimination in Mississippi and in Indiana. I felt raw hate. It was for me the most intense confrontation with racism that I ever experienced.

August 6, 1964

I paired up with Chris Wilson, a Stanford sophomore, in a voter registration team. We knocked on doors all forenoon. The sun was hot. We received a friendly reception, often with the words, "Here come the freedom workers." One woman we registered for the Democratic Freedom Party didn't know how old she was and couldn't write her name but her spirit was as strong as steel. We tasted some of the hate whites express here. As we arrived at a house two white furniture deliverers were leaving. Their actions and words expressed deep resentment at our presence. Several times a car with four white teenagers drove by. They cursed us, yelled "damn Yankees go home" and ran us off the road.... I felt fear as I moved into the white community but relaxed and safe in the Negro community. Why did this diverse group come to Hattiesburg this summer? A young woman from Oregon gave a good answer, "I came because I believe in an ideal and wanted to support it with my actions." The focus of this witness is Christian presence and identification with the oppressed. It appears to be deeply appreciated and to many it brings hope.

"Good News from the Graveyard"
Easter, 1964, Ebenezer Church, Atlanta

Martin Luther King fully occupied the pulpit.
His sermon, "Good News from the Graveyard."
Martin and the Spirit preached with great power.
The preacher said:
"The Easter story is Good News about God;
Good News about God's participation in history;
Good News about the reality of the unseen;

"Good News about death, death is not a blind alley
but an open door;
Good News about abundant and eternal life;
Good News about limitations of Caesar's power;
Good News that after Good Friday comes Easter;
We live in resurrection hope."
From the preacher's bench came "Tell 'em Martin."
A steady flow of Amens energized the preacher.

No, it could not be that an hour had passed!
It was the shortest long sermon I ever heard!
I joined the Amen Chorus and thanked God
for this fiery messenger of peace and justice.

August 7, 1964

My partner, a pastor from Illinois with teaching and counseling experience, and I visited a large white high school today. We thought we had an appointment with the head of the guidance department, secured on the premise that we wanted to learn about education and share some common professional interests. On arrival we were met in the lobby by a very hostile principal. His first words were, "We have no need for pious, self-righteous outsiders who don't know what the score is and who have plenty problems of their own." We quickly agreed to the latter and made clear we were not in Mississippi to give easy answers but wished to understand the situation. He said he would give us 10 minutes. Our failure to become defensive eased the climate a little. We indicated we were Christian educators. He responded by taking off on his own strong religious faith, his support of the church, his activity and leadership as a Sunday school teacher, as deacon, and as board member. Increasingly he became more relaxed even though his basic position did not change. Our coming had threatened and angered him, understandably so. Beyond this was a deep fear of how to handle a hot-spot school/community situation which he admitted needed changing, but the practical consequences of change really frightened him. The line between fear and hate is a thin one. Our listening and our efforts to understand his position made it possible for him to share his feelings more freely. At the close of the hour-long exchange he actually thanked us for our visit.

August 9, 1964

This evening five of us were invited to a Negro home about eight miles from Hattiesburg for a chicken barbecue. The place was quite isolated. The chicken and spare ribs were delicious, but the greater feast came from sensing the deep inner struggle and soul of these people. One of the neighbors present was the regional Vice President of the NAACP. He was deeply spiritual and very articulate. I spent considerable time listening to his story and his hopes. He kept saying how much our presence meant to him and his people. He placed emphasis on the risk

Northern whites were taking and how his faith and hope were strengthened by our coming. He said, "We do not hate the whites here because we know that hatred will kill our inner spirit."

October 12, 1964

Today The Goshen News *carried a brief item that made me angry and weep. The story said that hooded KKK men set fire to the home of the Vice President of NAACP near Hattiesburg and when he came out to escape the flames, he was shot and killed. How evil, evil really is! Witnessing against injustice is difficult and complex! Did my visit contribute to this Godly man's death?*

Excerpt from "A Celebration of Our Diversity and Unity: The day the KKK came to Goshen." August 17, 1996

We gather today in Shanklin Park to celebrate our rich diversity and to rejoice that God has created one human, rainbow-like family to which all belong. We also gather to raise our concern over this morning's visit of the KKK to the courthouse in downtown Goshen. We must speak and act against the evils of racism, prejudice and discrimination for they can destroy our community. . . . I hope and pray that some day history will record that on August 17, 1996, here in Goshen, Indiana, concerned Elkhart County people gathered together to celebrate God's creation, our human diversity and unity and to protest those who try to infect us with hate and fear. I hope the record will show that this gathering stood up for peace and justice for all, started a love flame and ignited a movement that changed the racial climate in this county and did so with joy and love. This is my prayer. I invite you to help bring this dream to reality.

Goshen College Response to Peace and Justice Issues, 1960s

In the 1960s Goshen College's awareness of the cancer of racism grew. How should the college respond? One way to discharge its moral responsibility was to provide educational opportunities for African-American students. Goshen College made special recruitment efforts and provided scholarships and other assistance to African-Americans. At one time this policy brought more than 60 African-American students to Goshen College. For a brief period in the 1960s Goshen College had small exchange programs with two Negro colleges in the South. Students from other racial and ethnic groups began to enroll. International student enrollment grew rapidly during this period.

We entered the 1960s expecting our "different" students to accept our values and our way of doing things. In time we discovered that our educational approaches, our pattern of accepting and relating to those different from us, had some serious limitations. We needed to learn from them.

Significant Innovation: Study-Service Term

In the mid-1960s Goshen College reviewed its mission and goals in the context of the changing political, economic and social world. An explosion of domestic and international violence and human need was taking place. How does the church respond to injustice, suffering and need? Faculty and administrators asked how Goshen College might better prepare students for Christian witness and service in this kind of emerging world. Under the leadership of the late President Paul Mininger and Provost Henry Weaver, Goshen College broke radical new ground in international education. After several years of exploration, serious study and two pilot units, Goshen College adopted the Study-Service Term in 1968, the first of its kind in the United States.

This service-learning program introduced students to cultures, problems, and achievements of the developing world and exposed students to cross-cultural settings. Every student was required, as a condition of graduation, to study abroad for a term or complete an international study program on campus. When confronted with the richness and diversity of human cultures, and the scope of need and suffering in the world, students reviewed and in many instances changed their priorities and life plans.

For me, the words of John Erskine express the unofficial goal of this service-learning program:

> *The body travels more easily than the mind and until we have limbered up our imaginations, we continue to think as though we had stayed home. We have not really budged a step until we take up residency in someone else's point of view.*

During the 1960s the draft, the Vietnam war, the women's movement and racism came to the campus. They brought concerns about faith, power, discrimination, relationships, education, meaning and authority. Students went to Washington, D.C., to protest the draft and the Vietnam War, they engaged Black Panthers in dialogue during several visits to the campus, and they took initiative in keeping the horrible conditions of war-torn Biafra in front of the campus community, the Mennonite Central Committee and the Mennonite Board of Missions. Students responded with anger, grief, conviction, vigils and prayers to the assassination of Martin Luther King Jr. in 1968 and to the killing of four Kent State University students by the Ohio National Guard at an anti-war rally.

In 1969 several Goshen College students, holding deep convictions that draft non-registration should be recognized as an acceptable peace position in the Mennonite Church, organized a student delegation that traveled to Turner, Oregon, to present their concerns to Mennonite General Conference. This student expression of concern was respected by most of the church leadership. In the late 1970s a Goshen student from Ohio was taken to court in Cleveland, Ohio, for refusing to register for the draft. The college administration and most faculty and students supported the student's right to take this position on the basis of conscience, rooted in his faith.

In 1973, growing awareness of world issues, and the question of our response to them, as well as a concern for the future of our historic peace heritage, led Goshen College to establish a Peace Studies program. What is the responsibility of the Christian in a torn and increasingly interconnected world? Is it to save souls or to work for peace and justice here on earth? While clearly both are part of our mandate, tension between these two poles has always existed within the Mennonite Church. Goshen College recognized that in order to prepare students for a changing world, these questions belonged in the curriculum. The establishment of a Peace Education Endowment in 1979 provided additional funds and resources to strengthen peace education both at the college and in the community. The realities and tensions of this period provided excellent opportunities to grow in understanding of how faith and learning at Goshen College relate to the issues, needs, problems and conflicts of church and world. It was an interesting and productive time.

Vietnam War, 1966–

Chapter Nine

Goshen College Chapel, January 20, 1966

That question came again, for the hundredth time. This time from a clerk in a hardware store. Why in the world are you going to Vietnam? You're not drafted–do you have to go? Yes! Let me tell you why. I am going to Vietnam because God calls the church and me into the ministry of reconciliation and hope-building. Christians belong where people suffer and where violence, hate, despair, fear, brokenness and chaos are pervasive. Love is the most powerful healing force in the world. God wills peace and justice for all. I will appreciate your prayers.

Beginning Questions

The Vietnam war raised many peace-related questions. How is relief carried out in a country involved in a civil war? In this war China and the USSR feed arms into the war machine of one side and the U.S. supplies arms and soldiers to the other. How does a relief agency maintain Christian identity and integrity in this complex situation? Is ministering to war suffering enough, or must the church try to stop the war? How does it do this?

At the request of Mennonite Central Committee, Goshen College granted me a leave from January through August 1966 to serve as the first director of Vietnam Christian Service. Winifred joined me in Saigon in April and became part of the

"Months to Replace"

Seventy helicopters destroyed
will take months to replace.
Ambush leaves eighteen dead
Heaviest raids of the war
Thousands of refugees
Millions of craters
Smart bombs destroy
peasants and soldiers
women and children
houses and villages
dikes and helicopters.
" Months to replace. . . ."
Replaceable ? ?

administrative team. This cooperative Protestant relief effort included Church World Service, Lutheran World Relief and Mennonite Central Committee. A half-page, seven-point memo provided guidelines for this new effort. MCC was asked to be the initial administrative agency. Mennonites had worked in Vietnam since 1954, were known and trusted, and were one of the Historic Peace Churches. Relief workers for Vietnam Christian Service came from various denominations and were sponsored by one of the three agencies. VCS provided emergency and development assistance to war refugees and others.

I hope the following sampling of journal entries, free verse poems, and commentaries will help the reader understand something of the nature of the war in Vietnam, its costs and devastating consequences, and how the experience made an impact on my peace and justice journey.

January 31, 1966

> *I just said good-bye to Winifred, our three daughters and close friends at the South Bend airport. I am on the first leg of my flight to troubled Vietnam. I must confess my heart cried as the plane took off. I am grateful, however, for this opportunity. I don't know what the future holds. This is a faith journey. It feels right to be going. I believe God wants me in this ministry. What else matters!*

February 10, 1966

> *Saigon faces look tired and anxious. Underneath one feels these are kind, patient and strong people who wonder why they are caught in this never-ending war. Yesterday's paper announced the annihilation of a Viet Cong company 25 miles east of here with an indifferent factualness in listing the number of enemy killed and structures destroyed. This suggests that blood and human life are indeed cheap! General William Westmoreland reported that Friendly Forces/ Viet*

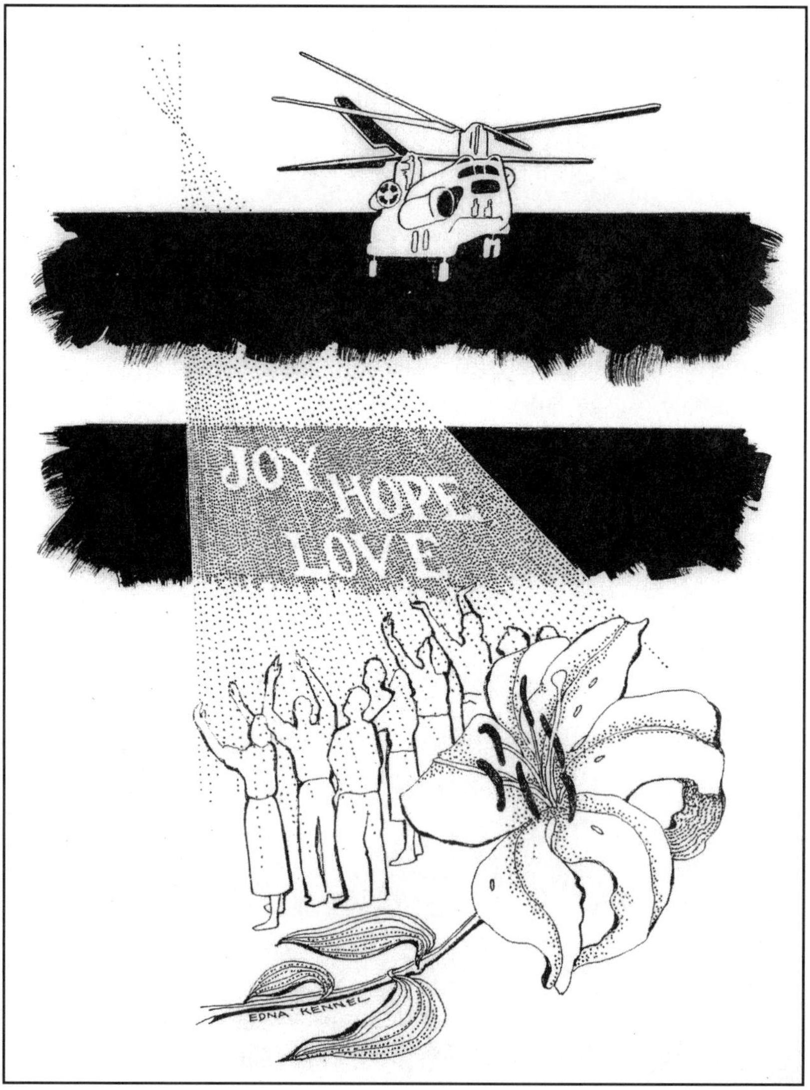
JOY
HOPE
LOVE
EDNA KENNEL

Cong kill ratio is more favorable this year, that fire and bomb power has greatly improved and that things are really moving forward. Sounds a little like what the French were saying in the 1950s!

February 25, 1966

While visiting Quang Ngai civilian hospital this morning, I went through the burn ward. Most of the patients were burned by napalm. Among them were two small boys who were horribly burned. An official with us said, "Yes, they are the innocent victims of the war." Indeed they were and thousands and thousands and thousands more! I wonder if this area of medical need–plastic surgery and related services for people burned by napalm–should be pursued.

April 3, 1966

A recent report states that the war is costing the U.S. $35 million dollars a day, and the estimated per kill cost is $375,000. The economy here is all screwed up. A shoe shine boy may make more in an evening than his father does in a week. The taxi and cycle drivers make high wages. The bar girls on Tu Do Street are in the highest income bracket. They may make as high as 70,000 to 80,000 piasters a month while the highest-paid civil servant makes 20,000 piasters!

Easter, 1966

Today is Easter. The cross and the resurrection are heavy and important themes to think about in this weary and troubled land. Twenty Vietnam Christian Service workers gathered in the back yard of the VCS house this morning to celebrate Christ's resurrection. It was a beautiful morning. In the distance we could hear the reverberating sounds of B-52s dropping their 60,000-pound bombs and closer in we could hear the continual noise of fighters and helicopters overhead.

Saigon, Easter, 1966

> In this weary and troubled land 20 relief workers
> Gather on Easter morning to celebrate the risen Christ.
> We sing the familiar hymns, hear the resurrection story
> And pray that the suffering and the killing will stop.
> The noise from the helicopters and bombers momentarily
> Drowns out the victory words of the resurrection story.
> The "flying chariots of iron" carry bombs and men into battle;
> Some men return, others become daily "body count" and "kill ratio."
> As we sing, "The Lord Is Risen Indeed, Hallelujah," the bonds
> Of death are broken, we are renewed and hope is reborn.
> Christ's resurrection warms our hearts, restores our souls and
> We rejoice and weep to be Christ's reconcilers in this place.

The United States dropped more than 25 million bombs on Vietnam. Death literally rained down from the sky. Beginning in 1962, an estimated 19 million gallons of Agent Orange and other chemicals were sprayed over 3.6 million acres. The medical consequences of these chemicals for humans, animals and crops are not fully known yet but appear to be great. Technology made available new, more impersonal and more efficient ways of killing and destroying. Soldiers who dropped the bombs did not see the suffering they created. In contrast, the war in the jungle and in the constantly shifting areas of military control did bring hellish immediacy to the killing. More than one million members of the Vietnamese military died in the war and 800,000 were wounded. No one knows how many civilian deaths there were, but some estimate that civilian causalities were three times as high as military causalities.

"Causalities Light" Saigon headlines

> B-52s Blast VC Concentrations
> Hotel Explosion Kills 28
> Search and Destroy Flattens 9 Villages

Black Market Disrupts Economy
Demonstrators Burn 3 U.S. Jeeps
Air Missions Destroy 23 Sampans and 94 Structures
Mined Truck, 48 Rice Farmers Killed
Self-Immolation Total 4
Buddhists Boycott Elections
Workers Mistaken for VC, 16 Killed
Kill Ratio 12 to 1 Favorable to Friendly Forces,

In the hospitals I saw the bodies of children and others horribly torn open by anti-personnel bombs and many who were severely burned by napalm. The empty bomb canisters read, "Made in the U.S.A." The war spilled over into Cambodia and Laos. The financial, human, emotional and spiritual costs are still being counted, and the billing will go on for many years. In addition, more than 55,000 members of the American military were killed, and 250,000 were wounded in this war. War is indeed hell! Today more than 20 million unexploded land mines in Vietnam, Cambodia and Laos lie in wait to bring belated death and injury to thousands and thousands of innocent people.

April 20, 1966

We had some neighborhood excitement last evening around eight o'clock. There were three substantial explosions shortly after A. J. Muste, long-term peace activist and head of Fellowship of Reconciliation for many years, and three associates arrived at the VCS house. The explosions sounded like they were just next door. This was followed by small arms fire. We turned out most of the lights. Some of our VCS workers and three of our guests quickly got under the heavy dining room table. Muste quietly said, "I'm too old to worry about my safety. I'm staying in my chair." I decided to keep him company. Later we learned that the Viet Cong were trying to blow up the police station about a hundred yards from our center. Muste is a tough old peace soldier. He and his colleagues want to contact peace people and at some point lead a peace protest march to the American Embassy.

Causalities Light

6 Hamlet Chiefs Assassinated
TB On Increase
Grenade Kills 5 Workers Waiting for Bus
Crops Defoliated
Friendly Village Mortared by Mistake, 89 Killed
Vietnamese-Caucasian Children Seek Foster Parents
U.S. Bags 814 Commies
10,465 New Refugees, More Expected
Body Count Today Totals 259
Bar Girls Demand Pay Increase
Civilians Lead Military 6 to 1 in War Causalities
Napalm Bombing Drives VC and Villagers from Hiding
Causalities Light??
And the people agonize and weep
Bruised and broken
Dislocated, despairing and weary
While the leaders ponder and check the body count
The people agonize and weep
And the wheels of war grind on and on...
Will it ever end?

April 22, 1966

> According to reports, Muste and his group were given rather rough treatment by Saigon government officials. The group started a press conference when the Vietnamese "toughs" started pelting the group with tomatoes and eggs while the security forces watched. At one point the security police took the delegation's signs and forcibly put Muste and his group into a paddy wagon and roared off to the airport with five jeeps of Vietnamese police leading the way. The Muste group kept throwing their peace tracts out the back window of the paddy wagon!

May 1, 1966

> The parade Sunday was anti-war and anti-American. The 4,000 to 6,000 participants were blocked by Vietnamese police from going to the American embassy. There were slogans and shouts, "Stop the war." "Americans go home." "You've made beggars of our children and prostitutes of our women." "We are tired of the war and we want peace." The opposition to the war is growing, particularly among the Buddhists. In the meantime, acts of terrorism and atrocities increase, people go on killing and being killed and the radio continues to report the body count and kill ratio as if they were baseball scores! When will it ever end?

June 8, 1966

> What is our task? We are the church at work in this place of suffering, death, dislocation and chaos. In the midst of this we are called to be the "fellowship of the caring."
>
> Acts of service must emerge out of a real sense of caring,
> out of a deep response to God's love.
> Our caring must be genuine.
> Our caring must be personal.
> Our caring must be sensitive to human aspirations.

> Our caring must be free from condescension.
> Our caring must not be used to make others feel obligated
> but rather to help others discover again a sense of self-respect.
> This caring is not deterred by hostility, by rejection, or
> lack of appreciation.
> This caring opens the way for hope to emerge and for the one
> cared for to start caring again.
> To live means to care, and to care means to live.
> This is our vocation!

July 4, 1966

> Doris Janzen Longacre made a strong witness for peace in this morning's worship service at the International Church. There was a fairly heavy dose of American nationalism and militarism present in the service. Doris was the organist. At a certain point Doris said she simply could not take the idolatry of nation worship. After two verses of a hymn that emphasized this theme she stopped playing, got up and walked out. She said she can't fully explain what happened except that she was over-powered with the travesty of it all. Later she had a good exchange with the pastor.

Vietnam Christian Service program decisions had human and political consequences. Church and state issues were involved. Governments tried to use relief agencies for their own political and military purposes. The propaganda war was clever and heavy. One widely known American evangelist visiting Vietnam said, "I have come to bring greetings from millions of Americans who are proud of what you are doing." The central message of reconciling grace for all people gets severely distorted when religious leaders claim God's special favor and support for killing for their side.

Mark Twain unveils this hypocrisy. He warns, *"When you have prayed for victory, you have prayed for many unmentioned results which cannot help but follow it."*

From "The War Prayer"

> "... If you would beseech a blessing on yourself, beware
> Lest without intent you invoke a curse upon a neighbor
> At the same time."
>
> –Mark Twain

To build an image that Vietnam Christian Service represents the church, not the American government or U.S. Aid, was a formidable challenge. I believe this goal was achieved to a considerable degree, though not completely. Of course, the battle was not fought only in Asia. The same questions were being discussed by Americans in churches and relief agencies all over North America.

July 20, 1966

> These past weeks we have been receiving important notes and gifts. Recently I received a letter from a family that decided to make the plight of the Vietnamese refugees a family project. Their daily prayers and their giving would center on this need. The 13-year-old son wrote, "I am enclosing with the family's money two dollars and twenty cents which I earned on my paper route. Dispose of it as you see fit. I plan to send a small monthly contribution to help the Vietnamese." Our Vietnamese baker gave VCS a check for 300,000 piasters for an X-ray machine for a clinic. Norman Cousins' encouraging letter along with a $25,000 check came today, contributions from Saturday Review readers to help restore the small village that "had been destroyed in order to save it," according to General Westmoreland. The mail also brought a contribution from the Union Church in Hiroshima, Japan. This gift carries special significance because of the massive suffering the people of Hiroshima endured as a result of the dropping of the first atomic bomb in WW II. There is an explosion of compassion taking place!

"Weeping Over Goshen"

I heard a 19-year-old cry,
a deep rooted, spilled out cry,
coming in uncontrollable waves.
No, she had not lost a friend,
or failed an examination,
or missed that special date.
She cried because a church in her town,
the white ushers of that respectable church,
told her and her friend to move along,
not to hang around their church.
Her friend was a boy with long hair,
they were passing out peace poems and songs.
"I can't understand it," she sobbed.
Can you?

July 23, 1966

Today I spent two hours with the managing editor of one of Saigon's major newspapers. What an informative experience! He is articulate, knows history, loves Vietnam and is critical of the Saigon government, the DRVN, the PRG and the U.S. He possesses great courage. Seldom does a day pass when there are not large blank spaces in his paper, the evidence of last-minute censure. He told me, "You Americans are making a serious mistake. You seem to think your values and ways of doing things are best for you and for us. You worship efficiency, progress, modernization, and freedom in the American sense. Our way of life holds different values. You think we should accept all of yours right away and that we should be grateful. We think we should be able to take the ones we want and take them at our own pace. We're anti-Communist too, and we need your help, but we are not fooled by your high-sounding phrases which say that you are here primarily to protect our rights. Our thinking people see through this and they resent your hypocritical attitude."

July 24, 1966

This morning I preached at the Episcopal Church on "God's People: The Compassionate Community." The experience was interesting and a little frightening. I lifted up Jesus and his life of deep, authentic caring for all people caught in the underside of society and then spoke of the suffering and the massive needs of the Vietnamese. I asked, what does it mean for the church to respond in compassion to the suffering in Vietnam and to work for peace? I didn't know U.S. Ambassador Henry Cabot Lodge and Mrs. Lodge were present until after the service. Mrs. Lodge had appreciative words for my message, but the Ambassador was silent. I was not surprised!

August 4, 1966

> I went up-country to visit relief projects. I was graciously hosted overnight by a veteran Western missionary. The next morning I joined him in a walk into the lovely country side. At one point he turned to me with these words: "The Lord has really been good to our side. The rains have come at night but the days are mostly clear. This helps our boys blast those Viet Cong. The Lord surely is on our side." I was surprised and troubled by my host's comments. I also was grateful for his hospitality and again thanked him for it! After a moment I simply asked if the church is dependent on the military to bring the Good News to the Vietnamese? And how will the Viet Cong who are killed in the raids hear the Good News? We remained friends!

Saigon, August 6, 1966

> After eight months here, I think of the indescribable confusion of Saigon traffic: the sound of B-52s dropping their bombs and of mortar and small arms fire; the continuing noise of aircraft overhead; the sight of helicopters bringing in the wounded and the dead; youthful Vietnamese and Americans dressed in battle gear ready to be airlifted into this war that has no front; the surprise explosions and the wondering that follows; the horribly disfigured in the burn wards of the hospitals; the number of children everywhere; the vacant and sometimes hostile stares of the old and the ill; the 23 bars on Tu Do Street; the smell of garbage-littered streets and the sight of children following American garbage trucks to see what can be salvaged; the crowded slum areas of Saigon; the flattened villages; and the immense war weariness everywhere.
>
> There are other impressions: the well defined Mekong River basin; the beautiful coastal area with its scattered fishing villages; the lovely highland and mountain regions; and the friendly, courageous people of Vietnam.
>
> –Excerpted from one of my reports. Full text published as guest editorial in *The Saturday Review*, December 3, 1966

August 10, 1966

> As the plane left the runway and headed out toward Hong Kong, Winifred and I felt a measure of relief. But an overwhelming sadness also swept over us, for the faces of the children and the old in the refugee camps, the hospitals and the underside of Saigon have been indelibly written into our hearts. No, we cannot forget them. In the days ahead they will return to haunt us, to drive us to do everything within our power to halt this great human tragedy and to urge sensitive people everywhere to reach across the world and help in the rebuilding of hope and life among these people. The troubled world groans in pain and my troubled heart gropes for adequate response.

Saigon, February 1, 1968

> At 4:00 a.m. we heard what sounded like bomb explosions and small arms fire nearby. Was this part of the traditional New Year's celebration? We turned on the small radio and heard that this was a major military offensive. The Provisional Revolutionary Government and Democratic Republic of Vietnam forces were attacking the American Embassy, other areas of Saigon and most of the provincial capitals of South Vietnam. We are confined to our hotel. The five of us are spending considerable time in Bible study and prayer for the Vietnamese and our workers and wondering.

> Looking from the rooftop of the Majestic Hotel, I see and hear the war. A large helicopter picked up a disabled one from the area directly east of the Saigon River. Several miles to the north, I can see planes drop their explosives and the dragon gun ships ready to go to work. South, toward the Cholon area, I see a similar scene. Heavy smoke pours upward from both areas. I know that military and civilian causalities will be heavy, and refugees are being generated before my eyes. A short time ago, a newscast reported that some of the most severe fighting of the war was going on all over South Vietnam but that everywhere government forces were driving the enemy back. "A very favorable 12-to-1 kill ratio" was being reported! The same

broadcast said there had been no report on civilian casualties but it is assumed they would be heavy.

February 5, 1968

Paul Leatherman still has not heard what has happened to the seven VCS field workers on loan to the World Relief Commission working in Hue. Hope is dimming for their safety. The fighting in Hue is reported very heavy. The Saigon VCS administration is trying every possible channel to secure information but has not been successful. The uncertainty lies heavily on the hearts of everyone. Paul reports all the other workers have been accounted for. I am glad Bill (Snyder) and I are here to share the load.

Today I flew to Nha Trang. The VCS medical team at the clinic was picked up by a U.S. military helicopter by order of the base commander and taken to the air force defense center when Tet fighting broke out. This was done without consultation. Our workers were disturbed by this action. After I checked in with the Nha Trang group, the unit leader and I went to the air base to talk to the responsible military officer about our concern. We first expressed appreciation for their concern for our workers. We then interpreted MCC policy of helping everyone in need to the degree possible and the uneasiness of our workers to be viewed as part of and dependent upon the military to carry out our humanitarian medical aid. We said we believe the PRG and the DRVN military forces know who we are, know what we do and respect the medical ministry in the Nha Trang area. We think this provides us with greater security than identification with the U.S. military. The officer appeared to understand our position. We received assurance that in the future the military would consult with our workers and respect their decision.

The traditional wishes at Tet are for happiness, wealth and longevity. A strange mixture of suffering, death, laughter, firecrackers, love, hate and despair has come to Vietnam during this New Year's celebration. This is nothing new here–but will it ever end?

February 9, 1968

The Hue team is safe! There was intense fighting near their house. The team reported they saw DRVN and PRG military a number of days during this time, but they left the workers alone. They may have known the humanitarian nature of the team's work. After the fighting subsided, American marines found the team. They were surprised to find American civilians and to find them unharmed. The marines took them by landing craft to Danang from where they flew to Saigon. Bill and I were moved by their story and impressed by their faith, spirit and courage. VCS is offering the Hue team and other workers the option of terminating or transferring to another country assignment if they wish. We are thankful for God's presence in this situation and we also weep for the hell and suffering that the war continues to bring. The team as a whole is responding to this tragedy with great maturity and compassion. They are recommitting themselves to the continuing task.

Ministering to war sufferers in post-war periods is always difficult. Problems are multiplied when relief is carried out when the country is engaged in civil war and when super powers use the war to fight each other. The complexity is increased when one's own nation is a major participant. All these conditions were true of Vietnam. And there is always the troubling question as to who has the right to designate certain people as our enemy. How do we express love and concern for those so classified? Jesus, Menno Simons, Tolstoy, Gandhi, Martin L. King Jr. and Walter Wink agree that we must love the enemy!

I spent four weeks in the summer of 1968 and again in the summer of 1970 visiting embassy officials of the Provisional Revolutionary Government and the Democratic Republic of Vietnam. These governments were supported by the USSR and the People's Republic of China while the U.S. poured millions of dollars in support of the Saigon government in the 1950s and then became deeply involved in military action in the '60s and early '70s. The purpose of my two summer assignments was to express MCC's concern for people living under "enemy" governments, explore possible ways to assist them, interpret

MCC's relief policy to help all people in need and present MCC's opposition to all wars.

A way was found to provide limited medical assistance to the people in North Vietnam and those living in Provisional Revolutionary Government areas. Trying to help all people in need during the fluid Vietnam war, however, was difficult and carried considerable risk. A number of VCS workers had deep convictions about this matter and creatively reached out to all factions in their geographic areas to the degree possible. Three Americans and one Japanese relief worker remained in Vietnam during and after the fall of the Saigon government and the takeover by the new communist government on April 30, 1975. The last Mennonite worker, Yoshihiro Ichikawa, left Saigon in September 1976. Earl Martin, one of the men who stayed, tells this dramatic story in his book, *Reaching For The Other Side*. Identification with the Vietnamese and their needs during this difficult time gave a measure of authenticity to MCC stated policy.

> In the summer of 1968 I had a significant three and a half-hour conversation with a Provisional Revolutionary Government embassy official in Prague. The first hour followed the usual pattern of polite exchange in more or less predictable political language. He then told me about his family, the people of his village and the impact of the war on them. He asked questions about Mennonites and what they believed about violence, war and peace, about my family and about life in Goshen. As we continued to share our stories, we discovered much common human ground in the similarities of our interests, needs and hopes.
>
> At one point he said, "There seems to be a strange paradox here. We have discovered common feelings of humanness and sympathy between us, and yet we are supposed to be at war with each other." His final words were, "After this terrible war is over, please come to visit me in my village for you are my friend. I would be glad to have Mennonites help in the rebuilding of my village."

May 21, 1971

> Ted Studebaker, a Church of the Brethren volunteer, was a gentle, effective agricultural peacemaker working with Vietnam Christian Service. I was blessed and challenged by his spirit and witness. He was loved and respected by those he served. In April 1971 he was killed by Vietnamese military forces. In a letter to his parents several weeks before he was killed, Ted wrote, "Above all, Christ taught me to love all people, including enemies, and to return good for evil, and that all men are brothers in Christ. I condemn all war and conscientiously refuse to take part in it. . . . I believe love is a stronger and more enduring power than hatred for my fellow men, regardless of who they are or what they believe." Ted gave his life for his faith. Ted's powerful witness for peace continues to speak to the world and to me.

A Related Memory

> Ted Studebaker's death reminds me of another Vietnam relief worker who became a war casualty. MCC worker Daniel Gerber, while serving in a Christian and Missionary Alliance leprosarium, was abducted by Vietnamese military forces on May 30, 1962. Daniel and two CMA workers who also were captured that evening disappeared and have not been seen or heard from since. Daniel spent one year at Goshen College in late 1950. I learned to know and appreciate his quiet spirit, keen mind and his deep peace and service convictions. He lived out Goshen College's motto, "Culture for Service." His life and spirit live on! Peacemaking may be costly.

"Vietnamization Is Succeeding"

To change the color of the corpses,
To save American lives.
The situation is well in hand;
The war has been programmed,
The computer needs feeding.
We arm the friendly forces—
Grenades, bombs, and bullets.
They arm the unfriendly forces.
Death drops from the sky,
Grenades, bombs, and bullets.
Death lurks in the jungle.
Brown is the color of the civilian dead,
Increasingly brown are the soldiers dead.
But the blood of the dead is always red.
Villages are uprooted, peasants live in fear,
The rich become fat, the people cry for peace.
But the war course is set to run on and on.
Advanced technology destroys land and people. Its efficiency
will bring quiet emptiness to the land.
Vietnamizaton is succeeding?

April 17, 1972 Letter to President Richard Nixon

Dear President Nixon:

Your words last night frightened me! You talked of the enemy shelling innocent civilians in villages.
God forgive us for the killing we have done with 26 million bombs.
You talked of a massive invasion of Vietnam.
> *Do you remember Cambodia and Laos?*

You asked us to look at the record, the reduction of U.S. ground troops.
> *You didn't mention the automated war and the increase in naval and air power.*

You mentioned the decrease in American dead.
> *You didn't say that the killing of South Vietnamese military and civilian reached a new high last week.*

You condemned "big powers" supplying sophiscated arms to carry out wars of aggression.
> *You didn't acknowledge our own soiled hands.*

You asked us to come together.
> *You didn't say that 75 percent of us are together.*

You talked about the danger of communist aggression.
In Beijing you talked of co-existence in spite of differences.
You talked of teaching the world that liberation wars do not pay.
Earlier you said that the U.S. world policeman role is over.
You talked of visiting 18 countries and finding great respect for America
and the Office of the President.
> *You didn't acknowledge the increasing fear and hate that millions feel toward America and the growing disillusionment about America's idealism and policies.*

You talked about a potential "blood bath."
> *You didn't mention the "blood flow" that has been going on for years and years.*

You talked about keeping the duly elected government in power.
> *You didn't say how that government got into power.*

"Hardening of the Arteries"

Three hundred sorties . . . great success
    Planes return without loss.
Eight hundred bombs dropped on Citadel.
    Viets move 50 yards inside.
Counter attack on Quang Tri,
    98 killed, 70 structures destroyed.
Exploding mine hits bus,
    23 die, many injured.
Bombs flatten village,
    "destroyed in order to save it."
Saigon cracks down on peace demonstrators,
    Students imprisoned and tortured.
Weekly military body count,
    North Vietnamese 3204
    South Vietnamese 623, U.S. 2
Weekly civilian dead–unknown
    Vietnamization succeeding?
Super power-National honor
    Bomb them back to the stone age.

War is hell. I've had enough!
I weep for the suffering everywhere.
Compassion fatigue is setting in.
God, let me not turn away.
Refill my compassion tank.
Clean out my arteries.
Restore my heart-beat again.

You talked about the generous peace conditions you offered.
 You didn't acknowledge their peace offers.
Your Words Last Night Frightened Me!
May God help us all!

Atlee Beechy,
Concerned Christian, Concerned Citizen

I joined representatives from two North American relief agencies in a 10-day visit to North Vietnam. The Vietnamese officials received us warmly. They knew of MCC's role in relief work in South Vietnam, my 1968 and 1970 visits to DRVN and PRG embassies and MCC's peace efforts. They also had a copy of Winifred and my book, *Vietnam: Who Cares?* The story in the January 12, 1974, journal entry personalizes the tragic cost of war.

January 12, 1974

The official farewell banquet for the three of us visiting North Vietnam was held this evening. After many courses and toasts and the special guests had left, we had a relaxed, informal visit with the Vietnamese who had accompanied us during our 10-day visit. It was only then that we learned that the interpreter's wife, three children and mother were killed in the 1972 Christmas week bombings. I shall never forget his face and his words. He quietly said, "I hate those who made the decision about the bombings. I don't think they fully knew what they were doing, but I have learned to respect and love the Americans that I have learned to know personally and this includes the three of you."
The past hour I tried to bring together the Christmas message of "Glory to God in the highest heaven, and on earth peace among those he favors," and the terrible bombings that killed my friend's family, and I could not. I wept and asked for forgiveness for my country's actions in this place!

November 7, 1993

I remember Hanoi from my 1974 visit as fairly drab and quiet with many bomb-damaged hospitals, bridges, public buildings and houses visible everywhere. Little had been repaired. In that visit I was particularly struck by the creative transformation into flowerbeds of the two feet wide, six feet deep bomb shelters scattered throughout the city. Today Hanoi is alive with people on the go and energetically pursuing a modified capitalism. The scars of war are still visible in some places today but there is a measure of hope in the air. Pride in Vietnamese identity and culture remain but the eroding impact of U.S. self-righteous policies continues. Normalization is long overdue. Our own self-interests would seem to demand normalization even though fairness, justice, compassion and reconciliation argue much more pervasively for me. MCC's continuing presence here is very important.

November 8, 1993

The Protestant Church service began at 8:00 a.m. with hymns, scripture reading, prayer and a sermon on baptism. The 100 applicants for baptism were excused to change their clothes while 10 persons prepared the built-in baptism fount. The applicants returned and the baptismal service began with hymns, scripture, prayer and short sermon. The service proceeded in an orderly manner–applicants lined up, took off their shoes, walked down the steps into the water, were immersed, received a baptismal blessing, moved up the steps and out the side door for a change of clothing again. This part of the service was completed in 35 minutes! Communion was first offered to the newly baptized–a fairly diverse group made up of minorities, older persons and a number on the younger side–and then to the rest of the congregation. The communion had much meaning for me. There were moments of weariness earlier in the service, but suddenly I looked at the faces and hands holding the wafers and the cups and my Menno self-righteousness melted away. I felt accepted and that I belonged to this group of Vietnamese believers, a part of God's church that reaches around the world. I thanked God for this relationship. The church is much alive!

Several ironic twists hit me this afternoon as Mr. Kiet took us to visit the Ho Chi Minh museum—how differently history might have turned out if the U.S. had responded positively to Ho Chi Minh's request for understanding the Vietnamese struggle for independence and need for economic assistance. Minh quoted liberally from the U.S. Declaration of Independence in his September 2, 1945, speech declaring Vietnam's independence. But with no help coming from the U.S., he turned for help to Russia and China, Vietnam's historic enemies. Today communism is breaking up in the former USSR, and Russian aid is largely drying up. Vietnam retains a form of communism even as it seeks trade and economic assistance everywhere. In a prominent corner of the museum sits a model of the failed American Edsel car with an Ohio license plate. There must be a lightly covered message here!

November 9, 1993

Kiet picked Gordon and me up at 7:30 this morning and took us to Mr. Hanh's office where I was greeted with a friendly hug. Hanh is the link between the Vietnamese government and all private non-governmental relief and development agencies. I first met him during my 1974 visit. He spoke freely and with appreciation for past and present MCC connections and then outlined the work of his office, which has expanded greatly in recent years. He sees himself as a bridge between the outside world and Vietnam. He spoke of continuing needs. I briefly reviewed and expressed appreciation for MCC's 40-year relationship with Vietnam, our continuing interest in the achievements, needs and problems of the Vietnamese and our concern for the future. I emphasized normalization of relationships and further reconciliation. It was a good exchange.

Summary Reflections on the Vietnam Experience

The following commentary on the war is taken from the February 14, 1994, issue of *Newsweek*. The author is William Broyles Jr., former editor-in-chief who had served as a U.S. Marine lieutenant in Vietnam.

> *War is many things, but unfortunately it's not a careful bookkeeper. It wastes lives and treasure like a spendthrift heir. War doesn't add up. The ledger doesn't balance. . . . The images poured out: the Zippo lighter just about to ignite the thatch roof, the young naked girl screaming in the road, the wounded marines on the tank, the miniskirted singers full bore into "Proud Mary," the bodies in the ditch in My Lai, and the helicopter leaving the embassy roof. Finally, all of us veterans touching the wall at the dedication of the Vietnam Veterans Memorial. . . . It was for nothing. It was all wasted–all the blood and treasure and high technology, all the bravery and USO shows and letters home, all the families waiting for that telegram they dreaded, all the lost potential of so many young men and women who never came home. . . . It's time for old soldiers, old enemies and old draft dodgers to make peace together.*

Observing the terrible consequences of the war on the life and culture of the Vietnamese people for an extended period has had a profound impact on me. To assist war sufferers was important and right, but to stop the carnage and killing was the ultimate task. The Vietnam experience caused many relief workers to move to a more active anti-war position. When they returned home, they often became strong peace advocates and supported the growing anti-war movement that included many veterans who had been stationed in and changed by Vietnam. Robert McNamara in his book, *In Retrospect*, credits the anti-war movement with having an impact on his position and he believes the movement was a significant factor in stopping the war. The peace witness did make a difference!

For Mennonites, Vietnam was a wrenching and a maturing experience. We discovered that ministering to war sufferers was complex, demanding and sometimes ambiguous. Working to stop the cause of the suffering is an inter-related dimension of the peace witness. For us to carry out the former without being actively involved in the latter falls short of following Christ's peacemaking call. The task is particularly complex in the midst of the chaos, corruption and breakdown of wartime. Relief agency decisions always have spiritual, moral and political implications. Sometimes the lines are not clear. I believe, however, that Christ's compassionate community belongs in the midst of the suffering and the turmoil, to be Christ's presence, to be his ministers of reconciliation and healing and to protest the evil of war and violence.

When I returned home in late August 1966, my diary tells me I spoke on average three times weekly on Vietnam, wrote articles and many letters to editors, religious leaders, congressmen, the U.S. State Department and the President to protest the war. The killing continued. In 1968 Winifred and I collaborated in writing the book, *Vietnam: Who Cares?*, summarizing our experiences and deep convictions against the war. My passion against war and violence was informed and immeasurably deepened by the Vietnam experience. My interest in and concern for the Vietnamese people and for Vietnam and U.S. relationships are deeply embedded in my heart.

Some Observations from the Vietnam Experience

> Relief and service agency decisions and actions represent significant power, which has important political, economic, social and religious implications.

> Spiritual roots, agency goals and the philosophy of supporting groups are important for the identity, credibility and image of the voluntary agency.

The nature and source of funding and other support is important for the identity, credibility and image of the voluntary agency.

Agencies cannot separate compassionate actions from concerns for stopping the violence of war and seeking justice. Provision for witness to both dimensions is imperative.

Agencies run the risk of being used overtly or subtly for political or military purposes by our own government, by host country governments, or other special interest and power groups.

Agency personnel should respect the values, identity, hopes and culture of the host people; and the recipients must have active involvement in program planning and administration.

Building relationships and working for reconciliation in a conflict situation requires time, effort, patience, integrity and actions. Peacemaking is important, complex and often costly.

The image of the church becomes seriously distorted when leading religious leaders claim God's support for their side in the killing and rationalize the violence of so-called just wars.

Service is compassionate sharing of things, skills, and self with others.

War is hell and terribly destructive. I believe the church belongs where there is suffering, chaos, despair, and conflict to be Christ's compassionate minister and reconciling and healing presence and action.

The concluding words of my sermon in the Episcopal Church in Saigon on July 24, 1966, are my invitation to all who read this page to commit or recommit themselves to work for the elimination of all wars:

Perhaps the day will come in our civilized and advanced age when prejudice, hate, fear, violence and war will not only seem illogical and wasteful but also unnecessary, a day when tanks and planes become the plowshares of the paddy fields. In the meantime, God's people must seek to eliminate those things which cause prejudice, hate, fear, violence and war. They must, in reality, be the compassionate community translating into all relationships the eternal, healing Spirit of God. This is our challenge today. Amen.

Significant Photos

Atlee Beechy,
Goshen College senior picture

Winifred Beechy,
Goshen College senior picture

Columbus, Ohio - Fulton Elementary School students

Goshen College wedding,
May 24, 1941

Columbus, Ohio, kitchen duties,
1942

C.P.S. camp #20 Sideling Hill, PA, camp staff 1944
Ralph and Elizabeth Hernley
Alen Britsch, Winifred and Atlee Beechy

C.P.S. camp #57 Hill City, SD, 1945

European relief, MCC clothing distribution, 1947

Goshen College, informal student-teacher exchange, 1965

India Sabbatical 1960-61
Dr. Radhakrishman, President of India
Reception for Fulbright lectures, 1960

Beechy family in India, 1960-61

Beechy family, 1965
Judy, Winifred, Karen, Atlee, Susan

Vietnam Christian Service refugee assistance, 1966

Saigon
MCC Peace Section consultant, Frank Epp

Saigon, Vietnam Christian Service
Beechys and two Vietnamese staff, 1966

Three-week International Peace Seminar
Vienna, 1970

Chengdu
Professor Sheng (center),
Chinese history professor for
SST, 1980

China SST 1980
First Undergraduate exchange with Chinese scholars since opening of US-China relations

Seniors for Peace, Coordinating Committee, 1987
Winifred and Atlee Beechy, Evelyn and Carl Kreider, Ethel and Roy Umble

Reunion of Vietnam alumni workers, July 2000
with Pat and Earl Martin and friend

The Beechys, Greencroft, October 2000

Nigeria – Biafra Visit, 1969

Chapter Ten

January 12, 1969

Today I saw children literally starving to death in this terrible civil war. The Nigerian military blockade of Biafra is tight. The only travel and food life-lines into Biafra are the night flights from the island of Sao Tome. Airport landing lights are turned on for 30 seconds as the planes land. Nigerian bombers harass these operations by frequent bombings. I flew in with the returning Mennonite medical team of Evelyn and Wallace Shellenberger and Lynford Gehman. They work under indescribable conditions. Today I accompanied Dr. Shellenberger in visits to camps for severely malnourished children, many in the final stages of dying. I am overwhelmed by the suffering, my emotions overloaded and numbed.

January 13, 1969

To break the numbness of overloaded emotions I try to keep open to the human and humorous in my peace journey. It was midnight. I was on the darkened Uli (Biafra) airstrip waiting for the supply plane to be serviced for my flight out to the island of Sao Tome. Someone cried, "Hit the trenches, the Nigerian bomber is coming." I jumped into the nearest one only to discover I had landed on top of a Catholic priest. He graciously said, "Welcome to my humble shelter. Please excuse my crowded quarters." The shelter was two feet wide, four feet long and

A Lament

People
on the move
looking for a yam or garri
son, daughter or husband
and wondering.
People
in the camps
hope disappearing
despair ascending
imprisoned by hunger
fear and hate
and wondering. . . .
Children
sit and wait
life escaping
death overtaking
and wondering.
The suffering too much. . . .

four feet deep. We agreed that God's Spirit creates ecumenical gatherings in unusual settings! The friendship bond was strong. The Nigerian bomber's aim was good from our perspective, his bombs falling some distance from us.

Reflections On Suffering

My inner-city teaching, brief days in Mississippi, the college years, the counseling exchanges, observing suffering related to illnesses, accidents, natural disasters and my overseas war-related relief experiences have deepened my empathy for all suffering everywhere. These experiences also raise unanswerable questions. Earlier in my life I heard rather simple explanations of suffering, often given in a somewhat pious tone–the person's suffering must be God's will, suffering has some hidden purpose, suffering is God's punishment, or the individual lacks sufficient faith to be healed. The responses to suffering vary. At times those who suffer or their relatives or friends turn to bitterness, apathy, anger or despair.

I also have been greatly inspired by persons who respond to suffering and grief with great courage and spirit. Such persons have indestructible faith and are empowered to sing their songs in the midst of dark clouds. I vividly remember a worship service in Biafra. While children and others were dying from lack of food, a large congregation was commissioning four persons to enter missionary service.

I asked my Chinese Christian friend, Dr. Yu Enmei, what kept her alive during the 27 years she spent in a Chinese prison under terrible conditions, including considerable time in solitary confinement. She replied, "My faith in God and the resurrection, my knowledge of my body and my emotions and a sense of perspective and hope." Her capacity to endure physical pain, emotional abuse, hunger and isolation was a spiritual miracle and psychological wonder. On her release she wasted little time in self-pity and bitterness. In her post-prison period she returned to medical work, to translation and research and to

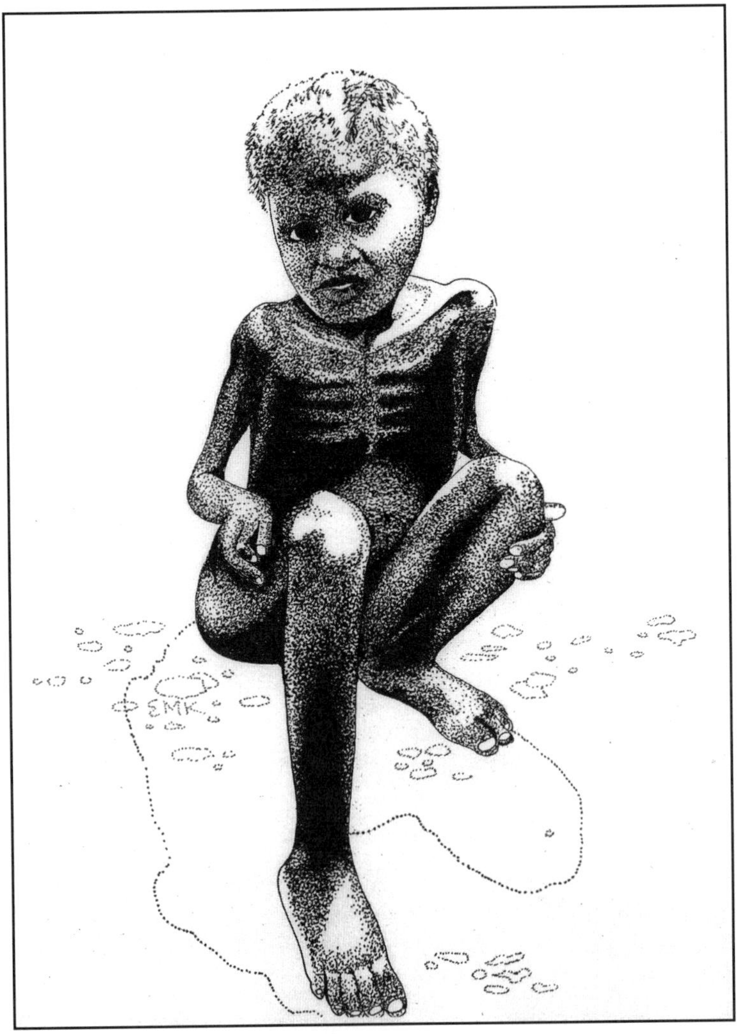
EMK

a pioneering ministry to the developmentally disabled. Her life is inspirational and instructive.

For me, there remains much mystery about suffering. I have no neat, pious answer to the why of suffering but I have come to believe that:

Suffering has many faces and roots.

God does not will suffering.

Holding on to our certainties—God's love and grace, love of family and friends and faith in the resurrection—strengthens our souls and sometimes our bodies.

Suffering may be instructive, sometimes enlarging our understandings, our empathy and our compassion.
Our choices and actions do have consequences that may lead to suffering for us or for others, but Jesus warns us against judging the suffering of others as being caused by their sins.

Suffering may be redemptive and transforming if it comes out of faithful witness and response to God's reconciling grace.

Prayer is a wonderful sustaining power in suffering.

God's unrationed love and comforting grace comes to us in the midst of suffering to minister to our souls, minds and bodies.

Most important, I have concluded that it is arrogant for me to think I can or should try to explain life's sufferings. I live with unanswered questions and pray daily for all who suffer.

I also remind myself of this message by an unknown author: "Do not feel totally, personally, irrevocably responsible for everything. That's my job. Love, God."

"Funds for Compassion": A 1970 Mission Board Call

Mennonites are the compassionate people.
They are known in capital cities and in the distant bush.
They respond to needs in Vietnam, Nigeria,
And 45 other countries around the globe.
They seek to help all people.
They believe in peace and justice for all.
Twenty million African Americans, six million Hispanic Americans,
one half million Native Americans, and millions of white poor
Americans—
These are the forgotten in this land of affluence.
They are the oppressed and the rejected.
They are the hungry and the homeless.
They are becoming disenchanted and angry.
The times call for awakening and action
The compassionate people have a goal.
Five hundred thousand dollars this year for needs here at home,
A drop in the bucket, but a start.
The effort is sputtering—more green fuel is needed!
Mennonites respond to world need,
But we seem blind to the agony nearby
Where are the resources for the Compassion Fund?
When will the money come pouring in?
Mennonites are the compassionate people?

China: Educational Exchanges, 1980+

Chapter Eleven

Eighth-century Chinese poet Tu Fu dreamed of a warless world.

On Washing Weapons

*While all scholars will write in praise of peace
and wise rule . . . I dream that there
might come some great man, who
would bring down the River of Heaven
cleaning all the weapons of blood,
so that they could be stored away*
forever, never to be used again!

Sichuan Bureau of Higher Education and Goshen College Scholar and Student Exchanges 1980-93, 1996+

Physicist Albert Einstein, whose research helped make the atom bomb, said before his death, *"The creation of the atom bomb has changed everything. If we are to survive we must change our way of thinking about our world."* Later he said, *"Peace cannot be kept by force; it can only be achieved by understanding."* To change our thinking patterns and to increase understanding is an educational task.

In the 1950s President Eisenhower strongly endorsed educational exchanges as the way to bring peace and security. In a 1956 speech Chinese Premier Chou Enlai said, *"We are deeply convinced that the day will come when the Chinese and the American peoples,* because of their traditional friendship, will resume their ties through their respective governments." And in May 1985 Donald Anderson, head of the China section in the U. S. State Department, stated, "Educational exchanges have been the most important single factor in improving relationships between China and the United States." I strongly agree.

China, where over one fifth of the world's population live, is important to Asia and to the rest of the world. Nations, like individuals and groups, behave in part out of perceptions they have of themselves, their role in the world, the role they see for other nations and the role which nations permit or encourage each other to play. The 30 years of closed borders and isolation were costly in terms of world peace. In those years distorted perceptions, national egos, political and economic interests helped create the enemy images that China and the United States had of each other. Both Americans and Chinese saw each other through a screen of cultural, political and historic biases.

J. Lawrence Burkholder, former president of Goshen College, dreamed for many years of a study-service program in China. His earlier relief experience in China in the late 1940s stimulated his interests and energized his efforts. Goshen College's SST program and the exchange idea appealed to Chinese officials. Burkholder's persistence was rewarded in December 1979 when he negotiated an exchange agreement with the Sichuan Bureau of Higher Education.

According to American Ambassador Leonard Woodcock, this exchange program was the first one between China and an American undergraduate college since the closed years. According to the agreement, Sichuan Normal University arranged an educational experience for 20 Goshen College students and two faculty co-leaders. In exchange Goshen College provided an academic year of English language and culture study for eight Chinese teachers of English. (In 1982 the numbers changed to 21 Goshen students and nine Chinese participants) Winifred and I were privileged to be the co-leaders of the first group of Goshen students to go to China in the fall of 1980. For us, and we believe for the students, this was a profound eye-, heart- and mind-opening experience that continues to have an impact on our ideas and understandings about the role of educational exchange in peacemaking.

How does an exchange program improve international understanding and build world peace? At the 10th anniversary of the Sichuan-Goshen exchange former President Burkholder said,

> *I would also like to think of the exchange as an attempt at peacemaking. This comes naturally to Mennonites since for centuries they have emphasized peace as their reason for existence. For Chinese and Americans to work together peacefully after their nations have been estranged with no diplomatic recognition for nearly 30 years is to prove that personal relations can transcend political differences.*

On the same occasion Wang Junneng, President of Sichuan Normal University, after noting a number of specific values of the exchange, concluded, "*The best of all benefits is, an extensive friendship has been established between our leading administrators, professors, teachers and students of our two academic institutions.*"

The Sichuan-Goshen College exchange has been given high marks by Chinese officials, by Chinese participants and by the leaders of the educational institutions from which Chinese teachers came. Marked improvement by these teachers in English language usage, teaching skills, educational leadership, and in broadened international perspectives were noted after the exchange year at Goshen College. In 1980 I gave an evaluation form to 270 Chinese students who were learning English from Goshen College students. In response to the question, "What were the most important things you learned from your American teachers?" Chinese students listed English language and American culture. In addition, the traits the Chinese most appreciated in their teachers were friendliness, kindness, openness, personal interest, genuine concern, enthusiasm, conscientiousness, modesty, fairness and their encouraging spirit. On a national English language test Chinese students who had Goshen teachers received exceptionally high marks. Other evaluations indicated that Goshen students increased significantly in learnings about China and Chinese culture, grew in personal development, and significantly broadened and deepened their international perspective.

Each Chinese teacher-scholar was given a Goshen host family with whom to share knowledge and experiences and for strengthening Chinese-American friendship. The bonding was strong. Repeatedly, in the final farewells at Goshen, I heard both Chinese and Americans say, "Now that we know each other as persons we have become friends and we can never again think of each other as enemies." Chinese participants and American host families gave this aspect of the program a high rating. Some participants still keep in touch with each other.

He Daokuan, a Chinese scholar participant in the first year of the exchange, describes his experience in these words:

> *In 1980 when I stepped on the soil of Goshen College campus, China and the United States had been separated for more than 30 years. The Goshen community and the American people at large had mixed feelings about China and us. But it soon proved that our American friends were understanding and understandable just as we were. They were curious about us and eager to learn about China. We were overwhelmed with hospitality and friendship. At that time we were considered non-commissioned people's envoys. We did our best to make up for the loss of time and the lack of interaction between our two peoples.*
>
> *. . . My year at Goshen was an eye-opener. My vision was enlarged, my life was enriched, and my knowledge was updated. I learned to know more about the humanities and social sciences. I learned to appreciate diversity and plurality of cultures. I learned to relate to people of various ethnic cultures and social backgrounds. My range of interests was extended, my intellect was sharpened, and my taste for scholarly work was refined. Thanks to my year at Goshen, I have been better able to teach both at the undergraduate and graduate levels.*

On the 10th anniversary of the Sichuan-Goshen exchange, student participant Lynda Nyce described the Goshen side of the exchange in these words.

During the past two months our group has joined the previous nine groups in learning about the culture and vast history of China. Through lectures given to us on history, great writers such as Tu Fu, Li Bai, Gomoro, Lu Xun and other aspects of culture, we can explore China's past and present. Many Goshen students have enjoyed Taiji Quan classes for health benefits. . . . Our journey began at historic places in Beijing and Xi'an and continued on the train to Chengdu. An excellent way to experience the sights, smells, and sounds of China; the windows of the train became our opening to mountains, rivers, endless fields, small towns and close communes. Another scenic highlight often emphasized by GC students is the trip to Mt. Emei over National Day. The majesty shown in full splendor in ancient mountains, flowing through clear and cool streams, and along age-old steps, refreshed us.

. . . Along with beauty, Chengdu is home to many GC friends. Each SST group speaks highly of friendships with students. The teaching experience has been greatly enhanced by contacts formed in class. Students are eager to have the Goshen teachers of English come to their dormitory rooms, look at pictures and inquire about each other's way of life. Goshen students fondly remember tines such as jiaozi picnics, English corner conversations and learning to dance Chinese style. The exchange is not one-sided in any way; we try to help our students learn English. In return, they extend friendship and welcome. Learning their way of life through conversations, shopping trips downtown, and asking any questions of our Chinese friends is a rare opportunity.

The exchange program between Sichuan Bureau of Higher Education and Goshen College operated for 13 years from the fall of 1980 through the fall of 1992 and brought 115 Chinese teachers of English to Goshen College for a year of language improvement and cross-culture studies. In return, the Sichuan

Education Commission and Sichuan Normal University provided a 14-week language and cultural studies program and teaching opportunities for 13 groups of Goshen Study/Service students. For the service dimension of the program Goshen students taught English to Chinese students in regular language classes. A total of 270 Goshen students and 26 faculty participated.

In a Goshen farewell convocation on April 30, 1993, recognizing the suspension of the exchange, Deng Hong commented:

> I am sure that what we have achieved here will become a rich source of motive and stimulus in our efforts to promote prosperity and understanding of the world.

At the same convocation the late Professor John Oyer, co-director of the fall 1992 SST group, said,

> We have been engaged in the most fruitful and durable bridge building: one person to another. You Chinese befriended us in Chengdu, Elkhart County citizens and people at Goshen College befriended the Chinese scholars. Friendships built in this way last a long time. . . . We have been happy participants in the task of helping to crumble walls between our two peoples, to build bridges instead. These Chinese friends will remain in our hearts for many years to come.

For financial reasons Goshen College reluctantly discontinued the program in 1993. Fortunately, Chinese and Goshen College officials, with the cooperation of China Educational Exchange, have developed a modified exchange program that continues to bring Chinese scholars to Goshen College and makes possible SST groups going to China periodically. In the fall of 1996 the first group of Goshen students went to Chengdu under the restructured program and the first group of Chinese scholars came to Goshen for the school year.

I believe the evidence supports the thesis that educational exchanges provide exciting educational and cultural learnings that have an impact on Chinese and American attitudes and behaviors in creating a more peaceful world.

What are the essentials of an effective exchange program? They are a built-in exchange component, a climate of mutual acceptance and trust, a commitment to emphasize commonalities and to respect differences, and the opportunity to experience each other's cultures in a direct, person-to-person way. Facts and knowledge are not enough to build the kind of peace and friendship bridges needed today. Without the experiential element, exchange programs do not reach the deeper learnings.

I hope the following journal entries from the first Goshen SST China experience will help the reader understand the dynamics of Chinese-American relationships and the human elements involved in this pioneer exchange effort. The experience significantly deepened my peace and justice convictions and my faith in educational exchanges as a way to work for peace in today's world.

Tokyo, August 26, 1980

> I wonder what our 20 students are thinking this evening. It seems unreal–boggles the mind. We are about to cross a curtain into a huge room where almost one fourth of the world's people live. We know very little about the country and the people. The past is now prologue. The now is here. We look to tomorrow and the days that follow with a mixture of feelings–eagerness and hesitancy, awe and hope, gratefulness and wonderment.

En route to Chengdu, September 2, 1980

> *This is Guangyuan, our first stop in Sichuan province. We have five and a half hours left on our 36 hour train ride from Beijing to Chengdu. We have come through the scenic mountainside cornfields of China and are now entering the rich Sichuan rice-growing valley. I am*

a little weary and a little anxious. What will be our reception? What will the next four months bring?

Later. *My fears were allayed by the friendly reception at the railroad station by representatives of the Bureau of Higher Education and Sichuan Teachers College, by the large welcoming banner which greeted us as we entered the campus, by the hot tea and snacks in the dining room of the new residence hall for foreign students, and finally by the comfortable rooms prepared for us. We are in for an interesting and stretching experience!*

Chengdu, September 6, 1980

Today we were formally welcomed with tea, fruit, sweets, many speeches, including a friendly, thoughtful one by President (and philosopher) Su Li. An official read in Chinese and English an extended list of regulations covering foreigners. I watched with interest the faces of our students! Next it was my turn to respond. I thanked the President for the very warm welcome that we were receiving, how honored we are to be in Sichuan Province, so rich in history and so forward moving in education, agriculture, industry and in arts and crafts. I said we have come to learn. The special lecturers for our group were introduced and a guest from the conservatory performed. Our students were asked to sing. They had been alerted. They responded by singing "This Land Is My Land" and "I Have Peace Like a River." The officials asked for another song. The students were not prepared for an encore. On the spot they selected the Menno national anthem, the doxology, 606, and rendered it with gusto and class. Once again the officials asked for another number. This time the students selected Jingle Bells and asked the Chinese who knew it to join in. A few did. What a mixture of compositions! This fits right into Mao's idea of life with contradictions. The President commended the students on the quality of their music and on their demeanor and spirit. I was proud of them.

September 10, 1980

> *Today we divided our students into two groups so that each student would have more opportunity to participate in the integration seminars. Winnie and I spent an hour with each group. Students shared their first impressions of China, their main frustrations and their primary satisfactions. The balance is definitely on the positive side. Main frustrations centered on being stared at, being over-protected and concerns about health. All are experiencing varying degrees of cultural shock. Initiating relationships with Chinese students represents both anxiety and promise. A recent volleyball game helped break the ice. Our students see themselves as unusually privileged and they are! It will be interesting to see how they handle the economic disparity and the political differences between our two countries.*

September 13, 1980

> *The health situation has improved. Last week we had three students in the hospital for two days. They received good care, though the experience generated some anxiety. Also last week we had 27 medical entries for stomach problems and this week only two! Was it the Chinese herbal pills the doctor distributed? They might have worked in spite of some skepticism!*

September 14, 1980

> *Students report that our dorm is called the Panda Palace. Over the long run I wonder if Chinese students will resent American students having only two to a room instead of eight and better furnishings. Officials keep over-apologizing about conditions here. And yet everyone seems excited about having new American friends. Sometimes when I comment on the warm welcome we are getting, the Chinese say "don't mention it" or "not at all" or "it's our duty."*

September 20, 1980

> *The students were turned loose to shop again, and they did! I am surprised and a bit shocked at how much they continue to buy. Today they made a run on water pipes, now made primarily for foreign tourists. What values do our buying patterns reflect to the Chinese? What does it say when we get more coupons to buy cotton than Chinese get in a year? One of our students made this perceptive comment, "We are a minority here but we surely don't act like it. We think of ourselves as being normal and the many thousands of people around us as strange and different."*

September 22, 1980

> *Our bearded friend, Professor Sen, who is giving our fascinating history lectures, joined us for our field trip today. He is an interesting character–strong, independent, alert, and personable. After liberation in 1949 the authorities cut off his beard. He grew it again. During the Cultural Revolution it was again cut off. They said it looked decadent. He grew it again, and again there was the threat of its being forcibly removed. He resisted and this time said, "No, if you cut off my beard, you will have to cut off my head as well." They left the beard on his face! When Professor Sen learned of my pacifism and my interest in nonviolence, he brought me a library copy of* Selected Poems *by Tu Fu. The poems are powerful, many strongly anti-war. "The Ballad of War Chariots," "Lament of the New Wife" and "On Washing Weapons" are particularly moving and compelling. I plan to pursue the nonviolent theme in Chinese literature and history.*

October 10, 1980

> *Dr. Yu Enmai, a friend of Dorothy and Don McCammon, visited our group today. She suffered horribly during the 27 years she spent in a Chinese prison, much of it in solitary confinement. Her crime against the state, that she had Western friends, including some Methodist and*

Mennonite missionaries. How did she survive? She spoke softly with deep emotion about the role of faith and hope in her painful experience. Dr Yu was released and officially reinstated into her medical profession in 1978. She is cautiously optimistic about the future of China. The church is alive. It will not die. It stands as light and "the darkness cannot overcome it." Here is a strong, indestructible, beautiful witness to God's grace and great human courage. Our students sang her favorite hymns–"Spirit of the Living God," "Abide with Me," and followed with "Peace Like a River," "606" and "God Be with You Till We Meet Again." She opened the window a little to the suffering she experienced during those terrible years. It was a high moment for all of us, including Dr. Yu Enmai. Our eyes did not stay dry! She agreed to come again.

Postscript, October 28, 1993

I visited Dr. Yu Enmei today, my fifth visit since 1980. Each time I have been richly graced and blessed by her wonderful words and spirit. At 90 she still works forenoons with developmentally disabled children. She believes old people should stay involved as long as they can. Enmei seems more frail than when seeing her in my 1990 visit. She told me she has lost 90 percent of her memory. She says every day she forgets where she puts things and has to search her apartment for them. I said I have the same problem. A few minutes later she asked if Winnie and I didn't give her a U.N. calendar in 1984. I had no idea! She got up, left the room and a few moments later came back with the calendar. We had a good laugh over her failing memory!

Enmei is pleased that her story, Tragedy And Triumph, has come out and is very grateful to Dorothy McCammon, Harriet Burkholder and Ruth Hsai for seeing it through to publication. I commented on the power of her life story and her remarkable faith and courage. She downplayed the latter. She said it was God's amazing grace, the 23rd Psalm, and prayer that kept her during the dark time. At a certain point she said with much feeling that she is very grateful for the Sichuan-Goshen College Exchange and for China Educational Exchange because important Chinese officials are impressed with these excellent programs.

The fact that we are Christian gives encouragement to Chinese Christians, particularly Chinese intellectuals. Both of us sensed this may well be our final earthly meeting but we knew that we were bound together in Christ's resurrection hope. I thank God for Enmei's life and witness and will be forever grateful for having been touched by her words, faith, and spirit.

October 16, 1980

Today I spent time explaining to university officials how Goshen College is church-related and how students look at their faith in Goshen and here. I explained our weekly internal worship service in our apartment and our rationale for it. I indicated our interest in learning about and if possible visiting a Chinese church. I said it was my understanding that Goshen students could respond to student questions about religion, faith, God and church beliefs and practices but that they would not actively try to persuade students to become Christians. I indicated many questions are being raised in the classrooms. The officials agreed that this was a satisfactory pattern. Many of our students are finding classroom exchanges interesting, challenging and sometimes stretching. In essence we are incarnating the theology of presence–being here as Christians in a relaxed and unapologetic way and responding to inquiries and situations. I plan to speak about religion in America in an up-coming Friday evening lecture and to include the alternate service provision and my own pacifist World War II experience in the presentation.

November 15, 1980

Yes, students are reflecting growth in their evaluation of the experience. A student recently wrote about her reactions. "We are expected to be good at everything. We are not always as open-minded as we should be. Too often we are concerned about our feelings and ourselves and not concerned enough about others. We too often forget our real purpose for being here in China and act as if it were one prolonged shopping trip. Too often we forget to be culturally sensitive. We forget to try to look at things from their point of view. But I think in the long run our time here has been pretty successful. They are getting to know us as individuals–seeing that we do have faults and insecurities. They see us as normal human beings just like they are. At the same time we are getting to know them as individuals. We are listening to their stories and their ideas."

November 23, 1980

Today we visited a commune where for an hour we were a production team. We picked 12 large baskets of oranges. It was fun. This was followed by a 10-course dinner and an extended rest period. We went back to work from 1:30 to 3:00 p.m., digging and cleaning sweet potatoes. The brigade leader was a woman who had 200 workers under her and knew them all personally. She was articulate and capable.

The evening brought a major surprise. Before we left for the commune I was told there would be several visitors from the American Embassy and they would take "pot luck" with us at dinner in the dining hall. We had no clue who was coming. At 5:45 p.m. Mr. Huang came to the apartment to say they had just received a phone call that U.S. Ambassador Leonard Woodcock and his wife Sharon were coming at 6:00 to have dinner with the group. They arrived and, after a formal welcome by the officials of the university, joined us for our regular fare with oranges from the commune for dessert.

After dinner we moved to our apartment for an additional two hours of delightful and informative exchange. The Woodcocks are warm, personable and articulate. They are deeply committed to China's development and to improving relationships between the two peoples. Leonard asked the students thoughtful questions. They responded well. They in turn asked about his assignment and his views on many issues in ways that reflected considerable understanding of China. The Woodcocks were much impressed with the students and the program. The students were impressed by the friendliness and the knowledge the Ambassador and his wife had of China. He is open to visiting Goshen College when he is in the U.S. We ended by singing 606. It was a large day!

November 23, 1980

In spite of important differences in cultural practices and political systems, what are the connecting points between Chinese and Mennonites? My tentative list at this point includes service to the people, upon which both Chinese and Mennonites place a high priority. Both place considerable value on family and children, on cooperation and group welfare, on education, simplicity, and work and on moral issues. We are discovering some common human qualities, needs and aspirations while recognizing and respecting differences.

November 29, 1980

This morning I typed the letter from the group to Premier Zhao expressing appreciation for our stay in Sichuan and inviting him to visit Goshen College if and when he comes to the U.S. Later, I had an exciting two and an a half hours with a Chinese psychologist from a nearby university. Zhang was a graduate of West China University and studied psychology at Boston and Harvard universities. His review of the role of psychology in Chinese culture and education was most interesting. Historically, China placed philosophy, psychology and moral development together as one academic discipline. Early Confucius writings raised some important psychological issues. Two of his students, Mencius and Zunzi, took sharply different views on the role of nurture and nature in human development. That issue remains on the agenda of many Western psychology conferences today. Zhang is enthusiastic about our exchange program. I gave him a copy of my psychology monograph and my paper, "Some Psychological Aspects of War and Peace." It was an instructive exchange.

December 2, 1980

This evening I had a high and a low. The high came from a wonderful performance by the Shanghai Opera Company of "The Flight to the Moon." The low point came from my feelings about expressing my irritation at not being informed about the program change until the last minute. There had been some accumulation of irritation from similar previous events. This time it was after 5:00 p.m. when an official brought tickets for the opera and said we are to eat at 5:30 and be ready to leave at 6:20. I released my frustration on the official and felt guilty afterwards because I knew he was not responsible. At intermission the official wanted to know why I was disturbed. I told him and he passed the information up the line. Later, I felt badly, not about stating my case, but for projecting my anger. I thought of the words of Jesus on this subject and also recalled the Chinese practice of self-criticism and confession. I wrote an apology and felt better.

Excerpt from my December 12, 1980, Apology Letter to the Head of the Foreign Affairs Office

One of the most important factors in transcultural communication, I believe, is the ability of people to "see each other's point of view." I try to practice this ideal. Yesterday, however, I failed badly in applying it. I apologize for over-reacting to you. . . . How do I know that my reaction was inappropriate? I saw it in the face of Mr. Huang. More importantly, I felt it in my heart. My response was not consistent with my ideals. Differences are inevitable, including those that build up unconsciously, but they dare not hurt our growing friendship. Today I confess my error, ask for your forgiveness and seek to restore and strengthen our relationship.

I had a courteous response from the Foreign Affairs Director. Perhaps this too is part of the peacemaking agenda!

December 8, 1980

Yesterday morning I had an interesting exchange with a Chinese student who has become a believer. He came to this position through his own reading and his questioning of his GC teacher. He said I gave some input in his class 10 days ago and that afterwards he asked me if someone could become a Christian without thoroughly knowing the

Bible, and I said I thought such a person could. The answer encouraged him and he started studying the Bible, attending the Protestant church and is currently reading Ferguson's The Politics of Love, a strong peace book. I listened to his story and responded to his questions. Who knows what the Spirit is doing?

Excerpts from My Remarks at the December 13, 1980 Farewell Ceremony

Respected Director Ding and President Su, lecturers and teachers, administrators, interpreters and students, we have begun a new venture. The night of separation has passed. The dawn has come. Phase one of the exchange will soon be history. We gather today to rejoice in our common venture and to celebrate its success. . . . All of you have taught us much about China and the Chinese people. We are deeply indebted and grateful for your interest in and loving concern for all of us, which began when Mr. Huang, Miss Wang and Mr. Yao met us at the Beijing airport and has continued to this moment. . . .

We leave tomorrow. We will take much more than the suitcases we carry. We will take new information, good memories, changed attitudes and perceptions, new understandings and appreciations and something of your spirit with us. We leave with you perhaps some new facts and perceptions of America and Americans, but most important we leave with you something of ourselves, our affection and respect, and a part of our inner spirits.

Last August on the large outdoor bulletin board near the administration building the students placed a lovely welcome message. It is still there, a little worn by the weather, but its message is clear. It closes with these words, "You come full of friendship of the American people and we wish you would go back full of friendship of the Chinese people too. Let's always be good friends." Please rest assured—we are returning with hearts full of the friendship of the Chinese people and we want always to be friends. Thank you.

December 13, 1980

Departure day has arrived. The past days have been busy with farewell visits and a formal dinner with huge amounts of delicious Sichuan food and equal amounts of mutually laudatory toasts! Most students are physically ready to leave and now are waiting until 9:00 p.m. this evening when we leave for the station. The disengagement is emotionally demanding. This has been a great experience. Its meaning will keep coming in on us in the days ahead. I feel good about what has happened, far exceeding our highest expectations. We made a start, a significant beginning. What this beginning will lead to only God knows. We have a wonderful group of students, and they did something which I doubt any other age category could have done. The students broke through to their peers in a personal, psychological sense and through this break-through reached the Chinese faculty, the university administration and Bureau officials. Last summer I recall a Chicago China meeting where a well know Mennonite leader raised serious question as to whether college-age students were mature enough to participate in an exchange program and handle the complexity of Chinese culture. The preliminary evidence sheds some light on his question.

December 16, 1980

The separation has taken place. I am reminded of Leon Uris' book title, Ireland, The Terrible Beauty. *In some ways the separation has been that—a terrible wrenching pain, but underneath there is the beauty of friendship, friendship of a nature and quality thought to be impossible to develop in a short four months. The first stage in the separation took place at 9:00 p.m. when the group left the campus. Many Chinese students and faculty came to say good-bye. There was some weeping by both Chinese and Americans as we left. More than 100 students, faculty and staff traveled the 10 kilometers to the station to see us off. In the ride to the station Winifred and I were in a car with President Su. Our discussion centered on the exchange and its meaning and its future. He seemed very pleased with the exchange and felt it was successful beyond his hopes. He added that the exchange had both a rational and an* emotional basis. Later at the station he saw the depth of the latter–the extensive weeping by Chinese and Americans. A solid friendship bond had been established. It was painful to be pulled apart! As the train slowly pulled out of the station, Chinese students ran along side of the train waving and saying good-bye, and American students responding with Dzai jyan, the Chinese word for good-bye. It was a never-to-be-forgotten moment!

December 17, 1980

We boarded our riverboat in Chongqing this morning at 7:00 a.m. for the 2,000-mile journey to Shanghai on the famous Yangtze River. Rivers of China have helped mark boundaries and shape military and political movements. The day is cloudy with some fog. Occasionally the sun breaks through. High, rolling hills provide boundaries for the river but sometimes the water overflows the low hills and serious flooding occurs. The fog blocked out our view of the first gorge. The sun broke the fog so that the second gorge rose before us in beauty and splendor. Periodically, we pass small houses and towns. The boat stops at the larger towns where some people leave and others get on the boat, often carrying many kinds of articles and sometimes small animals. The pilots who operate these boats must know their business for at places the channel is quite narrow and the rocks close by. The boat seems to serve an important transportation purpose for the Chinese along with providing a wonderful scenic and historic experience for a growing number of tourists.

Our first river seminar came off rather well. Preliminary plans for the January 28 Goshen College convocation were reviewed, modified and then approved. Students feel a healthy sense of responsibility because they are the first returning China SST group. How do we interpret what we saw, felt and learned to the college community? How do we do this with clarity, respect and fairness to the Chinese? A student committee is picking up the leadership for the planning. I know they will do a good job.

The second hour of the seminar focused on student reflections on the *evening we spent with a Western couple who taught English in a Chongqing university. One student criticized the couple's lifestyle and approach to witness. The ensuing discussion was serious and perceptive. The following questions were raised: What is mission? Who is a missionary? What are current approaches to mission? What is presence theology? Are we on the self-righteous side–quick to criticize but not having much to offer as an alternative? What is our purpose? Did we also take advantage of our American status in Chengdu–living, traveling, and buying? What are we doing with the new insights we now claim to have? I am pleased with these thoughtful questions. No, Winnie and I didn't give neat, clean answers. The conversation continues. We started individual checkout interviews today. These have been lasting about 45 minutes. We listened to student stories about the meaning of this experience. I was impressed with the quality of the responses of the six we interviewed.*

December 20, 1980

The river seminars are providing opportunity for two to four students to share, clarify and test their reflections and observations with the group. Seminar topics to date have been–Stereotypes, the Cultural Revolution, Re-entry, and Social Control and Morality in China and the United States. In the last seminar two students built their presentation around four propositions–that the Chinese are more honest than Americans, the Chinese are more ordered in their society than Americans, the Chinese are more sexually responsible than Americans, and the Chinese are more loyal to their government and to each other than Americans. This led to rather vigorous discussion with some differences of position. How does a society maintain moral standards and values? What causes societies to decay? What impact will modernization of China have on traditional Chinese values? What can we learn from each other?

Last night there was a beautiful full moon. The night has its own style of beauty. The wind is cold and raw. The river has widened. We see ships of all kinds and sizes as we approach the harbor. High buildings come into view. Shanghai is the gateway to China and serves as a connecting center to Hong Kong and the West. In our gathering tonight we listened to the old Christmas story, sang Christmas carols, prayed and waited on the Spirit. There was joy in our memories of Chengdu and joy in our thoughts of home.

December 25, 1980, Shanghai

Today is Christmas. The students and Winnie and I are celebrating the birth of the Prince of Peace in Shanghai. I think of the violence and bloodshed in the history of this country, in North America and the world, and I weep. I think of Christ's call to the ministry of reconciliation and wonder if our presence in China these past four months have contributed to building friendships and a more peaceful world. I think of Tu Fu's unfulfilled dream of a world without war, "cleaning all the weapons of blood, so that they could be stored forever, never to be used again."

This has been both a heavy and a joyous day. I sensed deeply spiritual moments when God's Spirit was as real as the air around us–last night when 5,000 people gathered for mid-night mass, this morning in our final meeting of the group, on the bus en route to the airport and in our final farewells to students. The accompanying Chinese staff and the two of us had misty eyes as we watched the JAL plane disappear in the heavens. Winnie turned to me and said, "They are gone. This will be the first time that we are separated from our students and alone since our arrival in China four months ago." There was pain and a note of relief in her voice! I thank God, our students, Goshen College and our Chinese friends for the gift of this enriching experience!

China: Teacher Exchanges, 1981+

Chapter Twelve

The Sichuan Commission on Education and China Educational Exchange

> *The success of this exchange program lies in our common belief in the great themes of peace and development. Our experience is an example of how people from vastly different social and economic backgrounds can work together and join in to promote world peace and human development. It also shows we should, and are, able to respect realities of other people's beliefs, systems and customs while pursuing the causes of our own choice. It is with the spirit of mutual respect, mutual understanding, equality and mutual benefit, which were laid down in the first exchange agreement, that the program has worked so successfully.*
>
> –Cai Li, Director of the International Education Office of the Sichuan Education Commission in "Reflections on Our Fifteen Years Together" in the *China Educational Exchange Update,* fall 1996

The student exchange between the Sichuan Education Commission in China, and Goshen College represented a major breakthrough. It led to the birth of a program for teachers, China Educational Exchange. This program was perhaps even more far-reaching in its impact. It provided a new model for the relationship between Chinese and North American educational leaders. Sichuan Education Commission officials made a strong plea for North American teachers of English for the 50 plus Sichuan colleges and universities. They hoped the program would include as well an opportunity for Chinese teachers of English to study and teach in North America.

Missiologist Wilbert Shenk gave creative leadership to the planning for the new program. He knew China mission history and missiology trends. In a study paper titled "Mission History and China," Shenk wrote, *"China represents the single-most important challenge to the Christian mission in modern times."* He concludes his paper with these words:

> *Whenever the Christian witness has resorted to "guns" to win a hearing for the gospel, the message has been violated and mutilated. Too often the stumbling block put in the way of those who are hearing the message of Jesus for the first time has been the stumbling block of arrogance, cultural superiority, coercion, or mixed motives on the part of the message bearer. . . . The goal in the communication of the Christian message is to help people encounter Jesus Christ and then make up their own minds whether or not to accept Him as Lord and follow Him in life.*

Shenk saw the invitation as an opportunity to provide a needed service, to take a fresh approach to being church in a socialist setting, to learn about China and to relate to Chinese Christians in new patterns of equality and respect. He helped shape the emerging theology of active presence and the CEE structure.

China Educational Exchange is a cooperative program of Mennonite agencies. Four Mennonite mission boards and Mennonite Central Committee form the basic support group, providing personnel and finances for the exchange. Mennonite colleges offer formal and informal teaching and learning opportunities and provide hosts for Chinese teachers and scholars. Chinese partners provide living facilities, teaching opportunities and supervision in Chinese colleges and universities and a salary.

In the summer of 1981 Goshen College organized and administered a successful summer English language institute at the request of Northeast University of Technology in Shenyang. On December 22, 1981, Robert Kreider and I reported to the China

Committee on our three-week visit to Sichuan and Shenyang. Chinese education officials in Sichuan and in Shenyang received us warmly and were anxious for the new exchange to expand.

The Sichuan officials were highly pleased with the personal traits, character and the quality teaching of the first three CEE teachers, James and Doris Bomberger and Elfrieda Enns. During the 1981-82 school year before CEE structures were fully in place, the Bombergers taught at Sichuan Normal University and Enns taught at Chongqing Teachers College. The officials also were pleased with the experience of the two Chinese professors who spent the 1981-82 school year at Goshen College where they audited classes, gave talks on Chinese history and culture and did some teaching. In 1982 CEE administered another summer English language institute in Shenyang. This experience led to the placement of CEE teachers at North East University of Technology in Shenyang in the regular school year.

I was asked to administer this new inter-Mennonite program and did so for the first year as volunteer director. Bert Lobe, MCC secretary for Asia, became director of China Educational Exchange on a part-time basis in December 1982. He gave strong leadership to the program for the next eight years. Myrrl Byler, after completing two years of teaching in Shenyang, became the third director of CEE in 1990. Byler continues to bring fine gifts and vision to the assignment. I continue to be involved with the shaping and development of this creative and exciting program. I officially served on the board of directors of CEE from its inception until the early 1990s. Since then, I have worked with the current board as consultant. One of my dreams is to celebrate the 20-year anniversary of the program with a conference in China, focusing specifically on educational exchanges, peace building and peace education.

What are the central elements in this exchange? This program, like the Goshen College exchange, emphasized trust, mutuality and respect by partners in the exchange. CEE welcomed the opportunity for providing a requested service, for learning about Chinese culture, including the church, and for building friendship with the Chinese people. The Chinese saw in the program opportunity for learning about American culture, for English language improvement, and building friendship with North Americans. Professional skills and personal qualities are important, and an active and secure faith are important for CEE teachers. Affirming commonalties and respecting differences are emphasized. CEE is sensitive to the dangers of new or resurrected forms of Western educational and religious imperialism. CEE respects Chinese Christians and churches and their goal of being indigenous and know that God is at work in China. CEE teachers learn much from Chinese Christians. They find great satisfaction in their teaching and learning relationships with Chinese students. Teachers normally go to China for two-year terms, but a number extend for additional years. Although the primary focus is on English teachers, the exchange also includes persons from agriculture, medicine and nursing.

Former U.S. Senator Paul Simons describes our world as "an exploding world, a suffering world and a world of too few bridges." CEE began in 1982 as a small but important bridge across which Chinese and North American teachers and others have been traveling. During CEE's first 19 years, over 200 North Americans have taught in China, and 90 Chinese scholars have spent a semester or year at a Mennonite college, teaching or taking classes. The exchange has touched the lives of thousands. A joint Chinese/CEE evaluation in 1986 strongly affirmed the program. Further reviews in 1988 and 1991 indicated that the exchange significantly influences Chinese and North American participants and that they in turn are having an impact on many other individuals and institutions. The program is having a positive influence on Chinese and American education, particularly in the areas of language, history, cultural studies and educational leadership. Although CEE teachers recognize major differences in culture and in political and economic systems, they also discover a common humanity that binds them to their Chinese friends. The exchange helps substantially to correct some distorted perceptions that each side has of the other, thus increasing mutual understanding and acceptance. The exchange stretches the mind, the imagination and the capacity to adapt. The experience often leads participants to review their life goals and planning and to see their own countries and the world in new perspectives.

The exchange provides an opportunity to relate to and learn from Chinese Christians. The Chinese church has had a difficult time and suffered much but remained alive during the post-revolution period and did so without Western missionaries. The desire for an indigenous church came out of the years of struggle and liberation. The church is growing. China Christian Council believes that Protestants numbered 700,000 prior to liberation in 1949, and today there are between 10 and 12 million members. The theology of presence calls CEE teachers to be Christ-like and to relate sensitively to and be supportive of Chinese Christians in appropriate ways in the situations in which they live and work. There is much to learn from our Chinese sisters and brothers in Christ about faithfulness, courage, suffering, hope, love for the Bible and healing if we really listen with integrity and humility to their faith stories.

Two commentaries speak to CEE's essential character. Zhan Xiaoyu is a student at Luoyang Institute of Technology. He writes about the impact of CEE teachers Margaret and Everett Metzler on him and his institute:

> Mr. and Mrs. Metzler only taught us one year, but our whole lives will benefit from it. They used their own actions to teach us the real meaning of life. Mr. and Mrs. Metzler love each other deeply. . . . Their life was very simple, but happiness was around them every day. Mr. and Mrs. Metzler love not only each other, but also others, especially their students. . . . Mr. and Mrs. Metzler treated everyone kindly and equally. We know that their affection for life stems from their belief: happiness is to help others. They never showed the advantages usually occupied by people in a commanding position. They always smiled patiently at the numerous questions and welcomed visitors. . . . They contributed money to a local church. They helped us arrange our international pen-pal activity. They bought dictionaries in the U.S. and sent them to us so we could further our study. Their love

and sincere friendship affected everyone around them and rekindled the same feeling in return. . . . We were eager to tell them our unusual or everyday experiences. We taught them Chinese poems. No one was afraid to talk to them. . . . They never spoke any vague or general Christian doctrines to us, but they themselves were the two best, most persuasive books, which showed their loyalty, and the Bible's great contributions to human beings."
—China Educational Exchange, Spring 1997

Ann Martin, after teaching two years at Chongqing Teachers College, describes what being in China meant to her.

Coming home has affirmed for me how good it was to go. It seems unthinkable that I might not have gone to China. . . . When I look around, I feel surprised that more of my peers haven't done what I did—break out of their routines and spend a few years in some far-flung corner of the world. There are times I envy them their master's degrees, their tiny but cozy families, their financial securities. Then the fruits of my labor seem uncomfortably intangible.

At such times I must look deeper to find out what difference China has made in me and whether it is worth what I missed out on. Beyond changed tastes and habits, beyond increased self- and cultural awareness, even beyond the ability to stand back and see from another's point of view, perhaps the most valuable change is that despite having come home, I can never again be at home in quite the same way. Before going to China, I knew the rest of the world was out there, but I didn't quite believe it. But now I know for sure that when the sun sets here, it is shining down on millions of bent peasant backs; shining down on millions of student heads, bowed over textbooks as they pace round their campuses, reciting; and shining down on millions of city dwellers commuting on packed buses and ferries to factories and businesses. This permanent awareness of "their" existence has given validity to both my going and my returning.

Retirement, 1983

Chapter Thirteen

During the 1983 winter term Winifred and I were invited to teach a course titled "The Peace Witness of the Churches" at Christian Theological Seminary in Indianapolis. I had worked with the dean on a Church World Service Global Education Committee. He knew my Mennonite connection and that I was a pacifist. The course was an interesting and stimulating experience. The nine students represented diverse backgrounds, including a veteran of military service and a chaplain from the Vietnam War-not the usual class mix we had been used to. This assignment did not involve teaching the already converted! The discussions were fairly intense. We learned a lot. We believe the students did too.

At the spring faculty/staff banquet in May 1983 I went through Goshen College's ritual of retirement-nice words and a gift. Appreciative notes and letters followed. GC had been the center of my life for 34 good years. My investment in-and returns from that investment-were substantial. I thank God, Goshen College, colleagues, students and my family for the richness of those years. To understand and work through the separation and grief took more time and energy than I had anticipated. Breaking the official bond really did pull at my heart, and underneath I felt profound gratitude and joy for my Goshen College years.

October 11, 1983
Reflections on Disengagement from Goshen College
After 34 Years

They were good years. Joy in learning about God and human beings. Joy in relationships. Joy in helping others learn and find their way. Joy in learning and taking help from others. Joy in working with wonderful colleagues in which love, competence, hope and commitment lived and found expression. Joy in the search for truth and change. Joy in witness to peace, human rights and faith. Joy and challenge in meeting conflict and controversy. Joy in the unexpected, sometimes the absurd and humorous and always in the warm human side of life. Joy in feeling needed and valued. Joy in sensing renewal within and sharing it with others. Joy in books, ideas, music, jogging, nature, games, retreats, stories. Joy in seeing students stretch, ask hard questions, declare themselves, move ahead in faith or sometimes start over. Joy in alumni living "culture for service" in all corners of the world. Joy in the daily encouragers–a word, a look, a touch, a smile, a question, an answer, a new commitment. Joy in feeling Christ's gentle and strong Spirit at work in those around me. Joy in God's call to the ministry of reconciliation–fighting injustices, hate, fear, conflict, despair, hunger with hope and the most powerful force in the world, God's non-violent love!

Mennonite Central Committee:
Akron, Pennsylvania, 1983-86

My major extra-curricular service activity has been with the Mennonite Central Committee. I was appointed to the MCC board in 1955, elected to the executive committee in 1961 and continued on the committee until 1982. During that period and beyond Winifred and I participated in numerous short-term MCC assignments. In 1983 MCC invited us to come to Akron for a year as "volunteers in residence," a nice-sounding invitation to come and make ourselves useful doing things that needed doing.

We accepted and came for a year and stayed for three years. For us this experience was a good way to make the break from Goshen College and to see if the college really could get along without us. They could and did. Another plus in the invitation was the close proximity of two of our children and their families. One lived in Royersford, Pennsylvania, an hour and a quarter from Akron and the other in Bordentown, New Jersey, two hours from Akron. The Akron service experience, and later part-time volunteer assignments with the Peace and Social Concerns Committee of the Mennonite Church, leads both of us to recommend highly voluntary service for retirees.

We joined the MCC Akron family in September 1983. We lived in a small apartment upstairs in North Hall. The capable and friendly staff took us in and made us feel needed and wanted. The constant flow of workers going out and returning provided a fertile growth environment. The returned workers shared valuable grassroots experiences and strong faith stories and convictions. International visitors introduced different perspectives and helpful insights into the discussions and planning. It was a stimulating climate and a fertile idea market place.

Winifred did research on certain projects, wrote articles and edited peace and other materials. She worked at rotating desks–moving to desks vacated by traveling staff. One year during Urbane Peachey's leave of absence, both of us worked in the International Peace Section. We participated in a review of Ron Sider's 1984 Mennonite World Conference peacemaker proposal that eventually led to the birth of Christian Peacemaker Teams. We helped plan and carry out a major conference on development. I served as informal consultant to overseas secretaries, to the Peace Section and to the Personnel Department. I also did some mediation troubleshooting and personal counseling. I joined Earl Martin and the late Bill Snyder in preparing a paper on MCC's approaches to working in conflict situations. I supported Executive Secretary John Lapp's efforts to make MCC's total program contribute to peacemaking and greater justice in the world. After spending considerable time in MCC overseas assignments, we found it was instructive to see how MCC's home base functions.

February 26, 1984

> The Akron MCC staff is dedicated and competent. They share themselves freely so that the "whole" may function effectively and minister in North America and across the world. They have normal human needs of being accepted, appreciated, and affirmed with some form of economic security. They also have normal tensions and frustrations. They are a community of God's servants doing ordinary and special things so that field personnel can carry out their ministry of compassion. I thank God for each one! The overseas secretaries carry very heavy loads. Their travel schedules, the number of field workers, the nature of their programs, budgetary factors, conditions in the host country and national and world political currents all impact their loads. Other influencing factors are their deep commitment, their pattern of administration and MCC's and their own expectations. These heavy demands also impact the families of overseas secretaries.

Since service is at the heart of MCC witness, I decided to do a little research on the basis and meaning of service. I drew on my observations and my own experiences. I asked outgoing and returning MCC workers to evaluate some beginning ideas and invited them to share their ideas about service. They made perceptive suggestions.

> Service is rooted in the disciple's relationship to Christ and to the person's voluntary response to God's grace and reconciliation. Service begins with being reconciled to God, to others and to one's self. Service may be misused to secure power or as an escape from responsibility. Service is an eliciting process and relationship. Service often requires long-term commitment. The goal of service is the total and ultimate welfare of others. Service is demanding and makes us vulnerable to burn-out. Service is a way of life, a loving spirit that penetrates into all relationships and situations. Service often means doing ordinary things,

sometimes monotonous tasks in a spirit of love and grace. Service is a relationship, a two-way process. Service is not so much doing something for someone as with someone. Service is hospitality–providing emotional and spiritual community and being fully present to others. Service is providing others the opportunity to serve you. Service is its own reward. Service is undergirded with joy, humility, hope, and is free from manipulative and paternalistic motivations. Service awakens hope.

This research will never be finished.

The Akron experience had three overseas blocks in it-four months in China, five weeks in Eastern Africa and five months in Ireland.

China Revisited, 1984

Winifred and I returned to China for four months at the invitation of the Sichuan Bureau of Higher Education in early February We were asked to give lectures at Sichuan Normal University where we had been in 1980 and at three universities in Chongqing. Winifred discussed American cultural topics. Her most popular lecture was "Seeing China through American Eyes." Parts of her 1982 book, *The New China*, were translated into Chinese and released in a daily newspaper in Chengdu. I gave lectures on educational and psychological topics. Since psychology had only recently been restored to the university curriculum, there was strong interest in trends and movements in Western psychology. The Chinese were particularly interested in personnel management, testing programs, holistic approaches to psychology and medicine and in research on one-child families. There were interesting discussions on nature and nurture theories rooted in Confucius' teachings and on the emerging role of psychology in modern Chinese society. I asked about the role of psychology in dealing with societal problems, including the problem of war and violence. A few saw a legitimate connection but others said that area was the business of governments.

Reflections:
My Last Visit to Chengdu

October 1993

I come to visit Chengdu, my Chinese home.
Here, in 1980, the Chinese people were born into my heart.
I come to remember.
I come to walk the old paths,
To enter the old gardens and buildings,
To feel the heart beat of Sichuan Normal University,
To see your new programs and buildings,
To hear your dreams.
I come to celebrate and strengthen our connections
And the people bridge that builds understanding!
I come with a full heart.
I come to have my heart stretched.
I rejoice in your significant achievements
And share empathy for the problems you face.
I join you in friendship and
In hope for a peaceful tomorrow.
I believe in China's future.
Farewell and thanks for the memories!

We also visited China Educational Exchange teachers and reviewed the program with Chinese officials who strongly affirmed it. They wanted to expand the effort. The officials took seriously our interest in being updated on the many changes in China. They arranged interviews with experts. We were warmly received everywhere and often with large quantities of wonderful Sichuan food.

We were accepted as "old friends" and reaped the rewards that go with that designation. Renewing these friendships, including contact with the courageous Dr. Yu Enmai, were highlights of this visit. Another significant experience was worshiping with 700 Chinese sisters and brothers in the Chengdu Protestant Church on Easter 1984. What a joyful resurrection celebration! We were renewed by the music, the preaching, the prayers and the spirit of the congregation, and the senior pastor, Daniel Li. This remarkable Christ-like brother lived in a very fragile body, but his spirit and wit remained strong. He is optimistic about the future of the church, unembittered about the past, and still creatively concerned about the present. What does he want from American Christians? *"They should keep us in their hearts and minds and pray for us."* I remembered our first visit to this congregation in 1980 when 70 people crowded into two small rooms. God is at work!

Another event stands out in my memory. Winifred and I see educational exchanges as peace and friendship building. We wanted to leave an appropriate symbol on campus. In consultation with the officials we selected two small pomegranate shrubs to be planted before we left and a pine tree to be transplanted later. The head of the nursery gave us "a sentimental price" for the three items and added, *"What a good symbol-the pomegranates for their flowers and fruit and the pine for growth and beauty in friendship."*

June 16, 1984

> This afternoon was farewell time. Madam Wang, head of the Bureau of Higher Education and Professor Wang, President of Sichuan Normal University, both gave flowery appreciation speeches along with gifts. I think they are genuinely pleased with both the Goshen College Exchange and with China Educational Exchange. I expressed appreciation for the way the two programs had developed. I emphasized peace and friendship building as a goal and a fruit of exchanges. Next was the planting of the two pomegranate shrubs. They were planted with tags indicating they were friendship gifts from us. They look quite nice. There were brief speeches about friendship and then the pictures.

Our daughter Karen joined us for the last three weeks of our four-month stay. She was on sabbatical leave the winter semester. She concluded that our invitation to family members to visit China was too good to pass up. Karen is a history buff. Her interest in Asia was ignited by our sabbatical year in India when she was sixteen. She found China fascinating and asked reflective questions. Her interest went beyond seeing tourist sites. To see China through her eyes and mind added an important dimension to our experience. She also brought the sad news of our daughter Susan's illness with breast cancer and helped us work through the pain and shock of that experience. Susan's positive attitude and daughter Judy's support and information-sharing role helped us maintain perspective during those difficult days. Our three daughters insisted we follow our travel plans. We finished our China itinerary but eliminated some other planned stops. The shadow was always present, but the Spirit and empathy from Chinese and American friends brought much comfort to us!

June 28, 1984

> The four months passed quickly. They were interesting and instructive. Someone has said, "China is changing very rapidly but a core of

Chinese culture never changes." Both are true! The economic reforms and growth are striking. They are beginning to change the consumer landscape and the economic motivation of peasants, factory workers and management personnel. Political reforms are not very visible. How long can this continue? However, the importance of China to the West and to the world has been underlined again and again during these months. How the United States sees her own role in the world and how she sees China and responds to China's aspirations, needs and problems are very important. Equally significant is how China sees herself and responds to the West. These factors will determine how violent or how peaceful the world will be.

For me the past four months have reaffirmed the validity of educational exchanges in themselves as a way to build a more peaceful world. The small bridge constructed in 1980 is stronger today, with increased two-way traffic.

Letter to Wilbur Birky, Celebrating 30 years of SST, September 7, 1998

I was interested in, supportive of, and involved in the planning for SST. I was on the committees that carried out two SST evaluations, one by external experts and the other by Goshen College and local area participants, including alumni of the program. Winifred and my field participation in SST was limited and had some different aspects from the normal SST pattern. We took the first group of GC students to Poland in the spring trimester of 1974 and the first group to China, the fall trimester of 1980. Each country had interesting and extended histories and cultures (one European and one Asian), and each had its form of socialist/communist government. Both were little understood in the West. The U.S. and these two countries together helped create a climate and a reality of isolationism for many years. In neither country did students live with families, but in dormitories. In Poland, students worked on state farms for their service, while in China they taught English in a Chinese university. The learning opportunities were great!

Eastern Africa, 1985

I was asked by MCC secretary for Africa and by the secretary for the International Peace Section to visit East Africa. My ignorance of East Africa was substantial. In preparation for the visit I read reports, articles and some books and talked to as many persons who had East African experience as I could find. What I received whetted my appetite.

My assignment was pastoral and administrative. I visited MCC workers in Northern Uganda as they reviewed program and reconciliation goals in the midst of growing violence.

I was briefly introduced to MCC work and church relationships in the Sudan, en route to Eritrea. The massive needs and sufferings of the Sudan generated by hate and civil war was then and continues to be largely ignored by much of the world.

Keith Gingerich gave compassionate leadership to MCC and ACROSS for many years in the Sudan. He was most helpful in orienting me to the Sudan and its pain and needs.

Eritrea was engaged in an extended struggle for greater independence. MCC responded to the suffering of the Ethiopians with relief and development programs. Severe drought, civil war and a repressive government for a period of years caused the suffering in Eritrea. MCC's relief policy calls for giving aid to the most needy and to help people on all sides of a conflict to the degree possible. Because of the civil war the primary way to get relief supplies into Eritrea was through the "backdoor" via a friendly Sudan. In response to reports that thousands of Eritreans had become refugees and many were dying from lack of food, MCC sent several large shipments of relief supplies to Eritrea, using the Sudan channel.

An important part of my assignment was to visit Eritrea and access relief needs as well as the goals, structures and programming of the Eritrea Relief Association. MCC and the MCC Peace Section also were interested in how war and peace are related to hunger, how to build on traditional African ways to resolve conflicts and how MCC's total program could contribute more directly to building peace. I turn to journal entries to tell the story of my Eritrea visit.

Port Sudan, February 20, 1985

> *I followed the map and walked the mile from the airport to the Eritrea Relief Association office. The office is a beehive of activity with responsibility for transportation of relief supplies and the planning for international visitors. Relief agency representatives and film crews are the dominant groups at present clamoring for attention. A medical clinic on the second floor treats civilian and military casualties and operates a very impressive rehabilitation center. There are many amputees around. One is sharing his room with me. He is cheerful and has a strong spirit. During my walk today I met two others who were learning to walk again. Both had lost legs in the war. One was singing as he painfully shuffled along. What courage he sent into my heart.*

Inside Eritrea, February 22, 1985

> *I am in a hidden away ERA guesthouse in the mountains of Sahel. It is a rugged, beautiful spot. It took us 13 hours and at least a thousand bumps to make it here by 4 a.m. Eight of us had considerable togetherness in the jeep. We stopped once for a meal of bread and a local curry. Delicious! Slept until 10:30 this morning, washed some clothes and had our first orientation session.*
>
> *At 4 p.m. we visited a general hospital 20 minutes from the guesthouse. The hospital is a series of buildings stretched along a six-kilometer canyon. For security reasons most are underground. The hospital has six major departments and treats 1,200 patients. There are 12 trained doctors. This hospital heads up the health care system for this region. It includes six regional hospitals, health centers for each 50,000 people and many village clinics. Self-reliance and having services as close as possible to where people live are key ideas. Medical problems center in severe malnutrition and infectious diseases, both*

aggravated by prolonged drought and the civil war. One-third of the children die before age one, one half before age five. They make 12 basic drugs here in the hospital, but medical equipment and supplies are very short. Transportation of patients to and from remote villages is a serious problem. I am impressed with the ingenuity and dedication of the medical staff and by their ability to stretch their meager resources.

War injuries resulting from napalm and personnel bombs became real to our group as patients caught in the bombing of a civilian market described their experiences. The two Harvard medical students in our group were deeply moved by this exchange and reflected their anger at the Ethiopian government for carrying out such bombings of civilians. I was glad to see their indignation but I also remembered what Americans did in Vietnam with anger and shame.

February 23, 1985

Today I visited a partially hidden school in a nearby valley. Three thousand pupils live in very primitive conditions and attend this school. The stated goal is "to produce dedicated citizens who will serve the revolution and help meet the many needs of our people." Grades one to seven are enrolled. The schools are skeleton buildings with a roof but no closed sides. They carry on with very limited school supplies. I visited classes in math, science and English. The teachers are dedicated and creative. Teaching and learning under these war conditions are very difficult. And yet I found the pupils alert, inquisitive and responsive. They are learning.

February 25, 1985

I observed a well-organized cooking oil and biscuit distribution at Sharit refugee camp. I noted the strong, proud faces of the old men; the women, who were mostly veiled; and children, many of whom showed serious signs of malnutrition. Visited nearby civilian hospital. Medical needs are very great.

February 26, 1985

> Today I visited Himer Refugee Camp. The camp is made up primarily of a semi- nomadic tribe, the Hadareds. I interviewed two families. It is clear their way of life has been totally destroyed by the civil war. The refugees are completely dependent on Eritrea Relief Association for basics. A nearby clinic operated by a "barefoot" doctor with limited resources is rendering a wonderful service.

February 27, 1985

> Traveled five hours over a mountain road that had 37 switchback curves to the Hivet POW camp. We had an hour's delay at the top because of a dense fog. This isolated camp houses around 3,000 Ethiopian prisoners. The prisoners constructed the facilities, primarily small stone enclosures with tin roofs. The camp appears well organized. I spent three hours walking around the camp with an interpreter. I was given permission to stop and talk to any prisoner I wished. I talked to 10 from various backgrounds. All were surprised at the good treatment they received from the Eritreans. They had not been tortured. I joined the prisoners for lunch. A highlight was a two-hour visit with an Ethiopian Airforce major, third in rank from the top airforce commander. The major has been in the airforce for 15 years and was trained in the U.S. and in the U.S.S.R. He was shot down over Eritrea in April 1984. He is Presbyterian with Mennonite connections in Ethiopia and the U.S. His personal journey story was very interesting and moving. In his spiritual and political journey he moved away from support of the war, and for this reason his family suffered. He was interested in peace questions and theology. I promised to send him some peace books, including some of Martin Luther King Jr.'s writings. I was informed and enriched by this exchange.

February 28, 1985

> *I visited the ghost city of Nakfa. It is in ruins, the result of a 1983 battle between the Ethiopian military and the Eritrean revolutionary army. Most buildings have been totally destroyed. The half-standing ones cry out in silence. The absence of any people adds an eerie dimension to the place.*

March 2, 1985

> *The Solomuna Camp has a refugee population of more than 10,000, mostly women, children and old men. Many of these had been in camps across the border in the Sudan, but when the Sudan made plans to move them into the interior of the Sudan, they came back across the border into Eritrea. More than 600 children live here, and many are orphans. I interviewed four women about living conditions. The conditions are terrible–shortage of food, three and four persons to a bed, limited medical services, isolation, no income–and yet they retain a measure of hope!*
>
> *Jonas and I have been closely connected for a week. He is my guide and interpreter. He is an interesting and able person and very knowledgeable about history and culture of this area. Our talk covered many subjects–governmental structure, independence movement, family life, religion, Mennonites, nonviolence, drought, tribal groups, education, economics, agriculture, food, medicine and the needs and aspirations of the people. Jonas is a non-practicing Catholic. A priest who had left the church led Jonas away from faith. Sometimes Jonas picked up my New Testament. One time he asked where God's grace and mercy are in the story of Lazarus. We had many interesting exchanges. He says he is coming to America some day and he wants to see Senator Ted Kennedy and visit Goshen. He thinks Kennedy might understand and help the Eritrean cause. Jonas talks like a liberationist within the socialist tradition. He uses such words as transformation and remodeling the system to bring about a free society where all are active participants and have equal*

opportunity. Jonas is friendly and a stimulating traveling companion. I learned much from him.

The week was intense. I have been exposed to great suffering and also great courage. My senses, mind, heart and body have all been stretched! I join the cry for peace in this troubled land.

Khartoum, March 3, 1985

Left this morning at five for Port Sudan. Stopped for four hours at a large Eritrean transportation and repair center. The movement of thousands of tons of relief supplies by trucks over rough roads takes a heavy toll on trucks and drivers. This center is basic to keeping the trucks running. I am impressed with the place. The center uses wind power for energy, has a tire re-capping department, and has machinery to make simple agriculture and cooking tools. A capable Belgium is part of the management team. We arrived tired and somewhat worn in Port Sudan at 10 p.m.

Port Sudan, March 4, 1985

Today I visited the Sudan warehouse where MCC and other relief supplies are stored. The large February MCC wheat shipment for Eritrea is here. It is in good shape and is scheduled to be trucked to the border within the week. Eritrean trucks then will pick it up and deliver it to the refugee camps. There is a current slow-up because of a shortage of fuel.

My senses and my heart are overloaded with the suffering I saw these past 10 days because of war and drought. My heart weeps. There is great need here, great weariness of the war and great longing for peace. I recall the words of Dr. Michael, public health coordinator for a large area: "We need your presence, your prayers and your food."

I flew back to Khartoum this evening. As we landed I saw Airforce One on the ground. Vice President George Bush is here for an official visit. At the guesthouse friends of the U.S. embassy staff reported that 400 advance personnel have been here clearing arrangements for this brief visit. Food and water for the entire group and three limousines came with the party. American awareness and a generous response to the tragedy here are needed and welcomed, but does it take all this for the visit?

Khartoum, March 5, 1985

I wrote a letter to U.S. Ambassador Horan on conditions and needs among refugees in the Sudan and in Eritrea. I also encouraged using U.S. influence to move toward a cease-fire in Eritrea on humanitarian grounds. The political issues are complex. I checked my letter with heads of several other agencies. I took the letter to the U.S. Embassy and talked briefly to the political affairs officer. Bush's visit is livening things up at the embassy!

Later I made contact with the head of the Eritrea Relief Association. He definitely wants continued MCC participation. He likes MCC's policies and approach. We discussed options.

While there I stumbled into a serious conflict between ERA and the International Committee of the Red Cross over relief supplies and policies for Ethiopian prisoners held by the Eritreans. Communication had totally broken down. The director indicated he would very much like to restore relationships with the ICRC. The ERA needs the economic help of the Red Cross, and the ICRC image is not helped by the conflict. I went to the ICRC office where I had a good discussion of its program and a frank exchange about the conflict with ERA. The newly arrived director of the ICRC asked good questions. He said he was troubled by the conflict and hoped to do something about re-establishing relationships with ERA. I asked permission to carry that message back to the ERA director. I delivered the message. A meeting of the two followed, resulting in the restoration of a working relationship. Both heads expressed appreciation for my role in restarting the conversation.

Sometimes peacemaking is simply being at the right place at the right time and doing a little gentle nudging for the parties to do what is right and what may also be in their own self-interests. In this situation I was the message carrier! The ICRC director suggested I stop in Geneva and give a report to his boss. I want to follow up with letters to the two parties involved. I will probably stop in Geneva at ICRC headquarters en route home.

Khartoum, March 6, 1985

How can I summarize these intense Sudan and the Eritrea experiences? I am too close to be objective. I also know the faces, the images and the many contacts will continue to haunt and to instruct me about the cost and suffering of war. But I try a first draft summary:

1. The situation seems to be moving from bad to critical to catastrophic. Refugees may total a million in Sudan. The Sudanese government is keeping an open door to refugees. The flow is picking up again, 3000 a day.

2. My teachers, the refugees who shared their stories and others who know the situation, agree that the answer for Sudan, Ethiopia and Eritrea lies in a political/social settlement, not a continuation of the war and violence that has been going on for so many years.

3. The church here sees service to refugees as part of its mission but seems somewhat hesitant to add peacemaking to its agenda. In Sudan Christians are left to decide if they will fight with the rebels, the government or flee and become refugees. One church leader is deeply concerned about the peace issue. He says, "Peace will only come when the people listen to each other and try to understand mutual needs and problems and to cooperate on common goals. Unless we do this we will destroy ourselves."

4. The Eritreans have kept alive a sense of identity, pride, history and destiny in spite of being exploited by the Turks, Egyptians, Italians, British and Ethiopians for many years. They continue to struggle for a measure of independence.

5. The Eritreans have a sense of community and common purpose, are organized with quite strong village level participation. They have the will and the skills to stretch their limited resources in amazing ways in education, agriculture and in medical services. But how long can the infrastructure stand against the violence of war and the drought?

Nairobi, March 7, 1985

I went to bed at nine last night and slept fitfully until the alarm called me at 1:15 a.m. I took the 3:30 a.m. flight from Khartoum to Nairobi, arriving at 7:30 a.m. At one point in the flight I looked out the right side of the plane and saw a lovely full moon and then looked toward the left side and saw the sun breaking through. What a wondrous sight! Harold Miller, friend and long-term East Africa peacemaker, met me at the airport. Spent the morning working on my Eritrea/Sudan report. My schedule demands me to shift gears, but my mind, heart and body need a little transition time.

Nairobi, March 9, 1985

East Africa country representatives are here for the MCC gathering. John and Alice Lapp have returned from a quick trip to Sharita. The informal exchange is beginning. Yesterday Harold and I had a meeting with the Reverend Mokono, leader of the Independent Churches movement. I met him in Lesotho in 1881. The movement continues to grow—more than 6,000 groups is his estimate. Peace is in their agenda but comes out of the traditional African culture ideas of order, harmony and the role of elders in settling conflicts. Had lunch and a good visit with Richard Ondeng, 1966 Goshen graduate. He is the deputy director of the Kenya Council of Churches, an important, though not an easy, assignment. We then spent an hour with Richard's superior, John Kaman, who described the work of the council and expressed appreciation for MCC connections and help. Later John Lapp, Harold Miller, Maynard Kurtz and I had a good discussion on MCC food policies and peacemaking and how MCC Peace Section relates. This is an important agenda item for the upcoming conference. Late afternoon Harold took the Lapps, Naomi Bender Shelter and me on a tour of the city. We saw the poor section, the market, historical sites and then the area where the foreigners live. Below the surface the impact of Western imperialism is still here. The contrasts are great in this beautiful city of a million.

Nairobi, March 10, 1985

I am fighting a bronchitis attack, am coughing a lot and didn't sleep well last night. Feel some better this evening. Tim Lind brought a letter from Winifred and an updated memo from the MCC Peace Section staff. This Akron touch served as good medicine! I rested this morning, hoping to facilitate the recovery process rather than going to church. I believe it helped!

The meeting of MCC country representatives of this region got under way this afternoon. After a bit of a slow start we got into the issues, problems and excitement of trying to link relief, development and peacemaking in this interesting, needy and somewhat violent area of the world. Harold Miller ignited discussion with his report that new research says the peasants have played a key role in food production where they were left alone and followed traditional agricultural methods. In other places, when new methods were introduced, often production increased initially but then dropped over a period of time. There are important implication in this for MCC workers and their work here. We are going to have an interesting time!

Nairobi, March 14, 1985

The conference is history. I was impressed with the quality and freedom of the discussions. These are able, compassionate, dedicated persons with a healthy sense of humor and perspective. The quality of the questions was high. Some of the underlying themes I heard included these: the complexity and difficulty of doing and measuring development, frustrations of daily existence, new ways to work with refugees, MCC objectives, personnel needs, networking and relationships with African churches and agencies, and the new pattern of administering in this region.

Many of these question have peace and justice dimensions, and these surfaced in a good way. What about the future of Uganda with its exploding violence and civil war? Is just being there in Christ's name and spirit enough? Are we called to do "peacemaking" in the chaos? If so, how?

I think there is some growing understanding of the food/reconciliation connection of MCC. Harold has developed an amazing network of contact—church, government agencies and non-government organizations. How the latter behave is a strong interest of Harold. He has serious question about food commodity use. He believes MCC must look at the deeper, long-term issues, including peasant farming and traditional African patterns of peacemaking. This means much sensitive listening and learning from Africans and their culture. John Lapp is empathetic to this approach. He raises reflective questions and works well with this group.

The last session of the conference focused on MCC's commitment to peace and how that commitment is/might/should be carried out in the programs in the countries represented here. I presented some MCC Peace Section materials and introduced the topic with this question: Do you accept the premise that all MCC efforts and programs should directly or indirectly contribute to building peace in the places MCC works? There was quite intense discussion after which there emerged consensus in support of the premise. Harold then asked, "How are you carrying out this objective in your programs? How can we make more effective the marriage of the peace imperative and MCC programs?"

The representatives shared what they were doing and what they would like to do if personnel and materials were available. These ideas surfaced: Cultivate the peaceable heart and spirit through disciplined meditation and prayer; plan conflict prevention and mediation education; study with nationals the biblical basis for peace and justice witness; be an active reconciling presence in the midst of tension, conflict and violence; actively seek local and national peacemaker relationships and gather traditional peacemaking stories, songs and symbols. For me, it was an exciting and productive session! These ideas may well become the foundation for a pamphlet I was asked to write on MCC's commitment to peace for use in orienting new MCC volunteers.

Nairobi, March 14, 1985

Yesterday afternoon Tesfatsion Dalellew, an Ethiopian Mennonite who works in planning and governmental relations for World Vision in this region, stopped by. He is articulate and well informed and frequently visits Ethiopia as part of his work. He is a cousin and close friend of the Ethiopian Airforce major I met in the Eritrean POW camp 10 days ago. The World Vision representative had just recently visited with the major's wife and family! He reported the wife was greatly concerned about her husband's physical and mental condition. She has had only one short letter from him since he was taken prisoner. Tesfatsion is returning to Ethiopia soon and hopes to visit the family again. He will update them on the major's condition and give them two pictures of the major I had taken. I am glad to be a small link in carrying important information between persons caught in the tragedy of war. God's Spirit does make interesting connections in unexpected places! Tesfatsion also reported that the church in Ethiopia is very much alive and growing rapidly.

Kampala, Uganda, March 22, 1985

Flew to Uganda with the Holsopples and Harold Miller on the 15th. Kampala was once a very lovely city, but economic, political conditions and the continuing civil war is taking a heavy toll on the infrastructure and the appearance of the city. We stayed at the Catholic guesthouse, comfortable and very adequate. The five-hour trip north to Hoima had some 20 army road checks. Some of the military checkers were very young. Several times we were asked for "something good" to facilitate the checking process.

Hoima is a city of 10,000. On the surface it seems quiet and friendly, but underneath there is considerable fear of both the "roving bandits" and undisciplined government forces. A year ago the bandits occupied the city for a day and then left. Fortunately, government forces were diverted to another area and so didn't have an excuse to plunder the city.

MCC workers stayed during this difficult time. Our four days here were filled with intense discussions about current problems of insecurity and violence, relationship frustrations with leaders and development issues and blocks. These factors seemed overwhelming. The future of the program was questioned. In the midst of this gloomy picture Mary Yoder said, "Yes, one can make a case for MCC withdrawing, but if we take seriously MCC's commitment to peace and look around at the massive reconciling needs here, then we must stay. I think it is time to move ahead on plans on how best to work for peace here." This was a pivotal moment. The group affirmed Mary's courageous position and agreed that the basic reasons for MCC's witness here are the following: to be an active reconciling presence; to observe, listen and report on the violence and the peace needs and efforts; and to carry on development projects to the degree possible.

The discussion reflected awareness of the complexity and difficulty of working for peace in this place. There is conflict between Catholics and Protestants, there is the tribal dimension (four major groups), there are political divisions, there is spiraling inflation and there are border tensions. When elections are announced, it seems the violence increases.

Religious persecution is not new here. In 1866, 22 Christians (Catholics and Protestants) were burned alive. A large Catholic shrine and a small Protestant memorial mark the place where this took place. The current head of the Uganda seminary told me the tragic story of the killing and raping that took place in the seminary a year ago. He spoke with tears in his voice but also with courage and hope about the future. I was deeply moved by the suffering and faith of my brother. The MCC workers are relating to this situation. They requested that the Mennonite Peace Shelf (basic peace book) be sent here.

My final contact in Uganda was with Kodwo Ankrah, a 1958 Goshen College graduate. He and his wife Maxine live on the Bishop College and Seminary campus about 20 kilometers from Kampala. Harold and I enjoyed their gracious hospitality. We were enriched by an informative and stimulating exchange that extended late into the night and again for several hours the next morning. Kodwo teaches several hours a week and carries some administrative responsibility at this institution but spends most of his time as Coordinator of Planning, Development, Rehabilitation and Research for the Church of Uganda, a very responsible position. He has been in it for 15 years. He believes MCC should be here in a development and reconciliation role.

I leave East Africa with a heavy heart. The suffering is massive. I also leave with profound respect for those national Christians and MCC workers who are working for peace in this place. May God help MCC to find a compassionate and helpful response to the needs and opportunities here.

Ireland, 1985-86

Chapter Fourteen

The Mennonite program in Ireland was jointly planned and administered by Mennonite Central Committee and Mennonite Board of Missions. Winifred and I were asked by these agencies to make a pastoral/personnel visit to Ireland in the fall of 1985. Our assignment was to study the situation in Ireland, review Mennonite presence and program since 1979, invite Irish Christians to help evaluate the effort and give suggestions for future planning. We also were asked to look at program goals, administrative structure and the nature and dynamics of inter-personal relationships of the group.

Vision for Mennonite involvement in Ireland came from leadership of the London Mennonite Centre, from an Irish Christian, Mike Guarde, and the Dublin mission/peace group, from the Mennonite Board of Missions and from the MCC Peace Section. For many years John and Pauline Fisher have been taking Goshen College literature students to Ireland. These experiences generated considerable interest in the life, people, history, culture and "the troubles" of Northern Ireland.

In December 1976, with the encouragement of the MCC Peace Section, I joined a 100-member delegation of North American church leaders in "A Journey of Reconciliation" to show support for the Peace Women and their efforts to stop the violence and bring peace to this troubled land. For me, this visit opened the window to the violence, pain and hopes of the Irish people and the complex causes of the conflict. Our words and presence didn't stop the killing. In the summer of 1977 I took my peace studies class, Violence and Non-Violence, to Ireland to study the situation firsthand. Irish peace and war literature and field visits became important resources for learning. John Fisher brought outstanding Irish resource persons to speak to his literature class. He often shared these speakers with my peace students. These Irish scholars and peacemakers helped us begin to understand the many dimensions of Irish culture and the "troubles" in the North. They also shared many stories of dedicated Irish peacemakers working to stop the violence.

Dublin, August 23, 1985

Greetings, Ireland. Your landscape looked beautiful as we flew into Dublin yesterday. Joe, Linda, Jacob, Aaron and Anna picked us up at the airport and brought us to 92 Ballybough, located near Fairview Park in north Dublin. This four-story townhouse building was purchased by Mennonite Board of Missions and Mennonite Central Committee in 1979, remodeled extensively and became the center for the new Mennonite work. Paul and Dawn Nelson came in 1979. Mike Guarde, Irish Mennonite, found the house and was involved from the beginning. Joe and Linda Liechty came in 1980. With the coming of children, physical and psychological space became more limited. How all of them lived in this house is beyond me, but they did for some time. The Liechtys moved to a separate location two years ago and the Nelsons a year ago. This place also is the meeting place for the Mennonite fellowship and for related programs.

Dublin, August 24, 1985

Today's editorial in The Irish Times *was very critical of Ronald Reagan's charge that the Russians were using cancer-producing powder for intelligence purposes. According to the editorial, the charge was not well documented and the motivation largely political. The U.S. wants to set the climate for up-coming summit talks. "O' would some power the gift give us to see ourselves as others see us." National self-interest* has many faces. I sent copy of the editorial and a note to President Reagan.

Dublin, August 27, 1985

Henri Nouwen's The Living Reminder *says some things that may be helpful here. Nouwen centers in on memory as pain source and hope generating. Memories can become a prison or they can liberate us. Remember God's love and grace is for all segments of a conflict. Spirituality and service are one. Being in God and being saturated with the Word is the beginning point of ministry. Doing emerges out of being.*

Dublin, August 30, 1985

The days move on. What am I doing here? I read The Irish Times, *watch certain TV programs and read books and magazine articles about Ireland. I am getting into some informal and formal counseling. I am gathering names of people who might share their impressions and insights regarding the Mennonite presence here. The group has touched an interesting, able and somewhat diverse group of important religious leaders. The "troubles" in Northern Ireland are of deep concern to me. I go along to do the weekly food shopping. I visited Paul's job creation project, the bicycle factory. Last Saturday Winnie and I explored downtown Dublin and bought a few items. I do my alternate-day jogging at 7 a.m. at a nearby park.*

Dublin, September 2, 1985

Sunday worship had a number of new faces, including someone who works with Irish students on Third World issues, a young man who returned after a period of absence and two visitors from London. Today Patrick Comerford preached from the story of the prodigal son with emphasis on the older brother and our problem of becoming isolated and discouraged with our own and the world's struggles. Patrick works for The Irish Times on international issues and news. He participates in deciding what stories are used and how they are developed. He is articulate and socially concerned. He says Reagan's reception last year was restrained. The Irish are unhappy with U.S. arrogance, with arms sales and with Central America policies.

Dublin, September 8, 1985

Ireland's economy is in trouble. The unemployment figure given last week is a new high of 17.5 percent. The farmers are hit hard by floods. Factories are closing or reducing their labor force. The new technology reduces the number of workers needed. Unions still carry some clout. The Dublin government gets most of the blame, though the British and the "troubles" in the North also get a share. Pubs and sports serve as diversionary ways to forget the problems. Gaelic football took over again yesterday in the nearby stadium where 65,000 fans gave vent to their emotions. Dublin beat Mayo in the semifinals and meets Kerry in two weeks.

Belfast, September 12, 1985

Belfast reflects two moods. People try to carry on daily activities as normally as possible but underneath I sense understandable tension and fear. People are busy in shops and cafés. I walk around the corner and meet British soldiers patrolling the area. There are slogans and other writings on walls, checkpoints and an occasional bombed building to remind me of the violence. This has been going on for years. Do the Irish ever get used to it? The Irish are warm, friendly, creative, strong, gifted, religious people with a sense of identity, history and humor. They seem to be held hostage by memories and historical interpretations. The conflict is fueled by extremist para-military groups who take things into their own hands and carry out surprise killings that lead to retributionary revenge. The cycle goes on and on.

I had a good exchange with David Blakely, executive secretary of the Council of Churches. He is a lay leader, radiates strong spiritual and human concerns along with a good sense of humor. His knowledge and love for Ireland cannot be missed. He shared excitement about the council's joint Protestant/Catholic peace education program. Blakely commented, "We know Mennonites, we know their approach, we like the way they work, we know their commitment to nonviolence and we are glad to have them around." I again met David Stevens who now is the associate secretary. In 1979 he visited Goshen College and spoke in chapel and to my classes. It was good to see him again.

I joined Joe Leichty for an evening meeting at the Quaker Center to discuss the need for another mediation center. The 25 persons represented agencies currently working in the north. After lively discussion the group agreed to have the executive committee develop a specific proposal and bring it back to the group at the next meeting. There is growing awareness of and interest in John Paul Lederach's elicitive approach to conflict management.

It was 11 p.m. by the time we got to Joe and Janet Campbell's home in Hollywood, a suburb of Belfast. We had a stimulating discussion on faith, on Joe's YMCA creative youth program with Protestant and Catholic participants, the "troubles" and Mennonites continuing until 12:45 a.m. Joe is an evangelical Presbyterian committed to social concerns and nonviolence. He would be glad for Menno volunteers. His program is aimed at witness and reconciliation. The Campbells are a warm, friendly, able and dedicated family witnessing and working for peace in this troubled place. We managed to make the 9 a.m. train and arrived back in Dublin by noon. This Belfast exposure was instructive and helpful.

Dublin, October 27, 1985

Today is my 71st birthday. Winnie cooked up a delicious dinner but reminded me not to expect this treatment every Sunday. I jogged four miles today in a nearby park. It is a lovely place to run, and you meet interesting people. Another "older" man asked me if I was running in the Dublin marathon tomorrow. More than 6,000 are participating. He seemed disappointed when I said no. This evening I read a good article by Bishop Ting on peace in China Reconstructs. *As I write this, I am listening to a tape of the Nanjing Seminary Choir singing hymns composed by Chinese, an important development. This has been a very good day. Life is a gift. God's Spirit is alive and moving here and across the world. His grace is amazing, comforting, confronting and renewing. My problem is that I don't take enough time to listen to the Spirit*

Dublin, October 29, 1985

Today Winnie and I walked to the Pax Christi office and spent two and a half hours with Sister Christina, the Irish director. She is a quiet-speaking, deeply spiritual, caring person. Pax Christi has 70 members and another 50 persons get their mailings. Sister Christina has been involved the past eight years. Pax Christi helped bring Gene Sharp and Ron Kraybill to Ireland for short visits.
Sister Christina strongly affirms Mennonite presence in Ireland. She appreciates the emphasis on peace and reconciliation, community and the approach Mennonites have taken toward Catholics. It was a good afternoon.

Dublin, November 4, 1985

I am reading Edward: Pilgrim Of A Mind, *the diary of Edward Yoder. What an amazing story of a liberated Amish/Mennonite boy whose mind and heart were captured by Christ and the classics! The human side of Edward's economic struggle, his efforts to be a scholar in the midst of administrative demands and his ambiguities with church leadership and structures all come through with clarity and emotional power. His dedication and commitment in spite of differences and questioning are remarkable. I found him to be a great scholar and effective teacher at Goshen College. His writings on the biblical basis of peace had a strong influence on me.*

Belfast, December 3, 1985

> *En route to Belfast we got a small taste of the threatening climate people here live with all the time. Because of a bomb threat at Central Station in downtown Belfast, all passengers were asked to leave the train at Lisburn. A local train was there, and we were told to get on it. It took us to Botanic where we were again told to detrain. Later we were told that no train would go to downtown Belfast. Fortunately for us, Quaker friend Denis Barrett learned of the bomb threat and came by car to pick us up at Botanic. After tea with Monica and Denis and a catch-up visit with them on their busy peace agenda, we visited the Peace Education Center at the Council of Churches. On Saturday Winnie and I participated in an important conference on mediation where the idea of a new peace center again was tested. There were excellent presentations from diverse peace activists. Sunday morning we worshiped God with the Quakers and were renewed.*

Belfast, December 4, 1985

> *Last evening Winnie and I heard Ian Paisley preach on "For whom the Bell Tolls!" His opening words: "The bell always tolls for the death of all traitors." His text, Numbers 32:23, "But if you do not do this, you have sinned against the Lord; and be sure your sin will find you out." What a hate-spewing and name-calling hour and a half it was! But it was instructive. Above the raised pulpit were the words WE PREACH CHRIST CRUCIFIED and on each side banners, Salvation to the Uttermost and Jesus Christ is Lord. Behind the pulpit was a good-sized plaque with the words, FOR GOD AND ULSTER. Hell fire and damnation were offered to those who differ from the elect followers of Christ. I heard amens coming from various parts of this well dressed and attentive audience. He gave an extended invitation to confess and commit or recommit to Christ.*
>
> *As I reflected on the service I wondered how often religion is distorted and used for political and power purposes–South Africa, the Middle East, the U.S., Ireland and. . . . Is this what civil religion is about? I*

wonder what spiritual and psychological experiences produced this fiery orator and political leader. Has anyone really listened and heard him out? What is he like outside the pulpit? As I watched him shake hands with congregation members after the service, I was impressed with the personal way he did it. But I still wonder why people accept his radical leadership. Are these questions related to peacemaking in Ireland?

December 5, 1985

Today we had good conversations with John Morrow, Corrymeela director, Sister Mary Grant, Gladys and Simon Bursch from Cornerstone and Joe Campbell of the YMCA. They are people with vision, dedication and great courage working on the grassroots level. I had a brief, cherished time with Carmel Heaney, student from Belfast who joined my peace studies class for a week at Glencree in 1977.

Dublin, December 22, 1985

I visited Maynooth last Thursday where I interviewed Enda McDonaugh, professor of theology, and Joe Lucey, one of his students. The latter has become seriously interested in pacifism and nonviolent action. He is looking at Mennonite peace theology and practice. McDonaugh gives encouragement for Mennonites to stay in Ireland. He knows and appreciates Joe Liechty and his important research and John H. Yoder and his writings.

On Friday evening Olive and Robert Dunlop were here. Robert is pastor of one of the Baptist churches in the Republic. The Dunlops are attracted to Mennonites because of their theology and faith expression. They encourage continued Mennonite presence here and would like to see expansion of Mennonite involvement in the North. They gave good counsel.

Yesterday Winnie and I spent a fascinating day with Brother Eoin at Balto Abbey near Noone. He is one of 15 Trappist monks who operate *a large dairy farm, spend much time in prayer and worship and run a small retreat guesthouse.*

Hospitality in the Henri Nouwen sense is practiced with joy and the presence of the Spirit. Eoin has been an excellent resource for the Mennonite peace/mission group here. His first connecting link to Mennonites was Yoder's The Politics Of Jesus. *Eoin found it helpful in writing a commentary on the Pope's speech when the Pope visited Ireland. Eoin's three-month visit to the U.S. earlier this year had substantial contact with Mennos in it. His interest in Catholic/Mennonite dialogue on theological issues is strong. Not all his co-priests are as enthusiastic. Eoin's daily assignment is taking care of the calves. In this peaceful setting we found both stimulation and renewal. I sensed empathy for the Mennonite group and strong encouragement for them to continue in Ireland.*

Dublin, December 26, 1985

This morning the Spirit nudged me to write to Ian Paisley and in the evening to George Alexenko, my Goshen friend. I don't know of any two persons anywhere in the world with whom I have greater differences on biblical interpretations of peace, justice and violence issues. Perhaps the Christmas Spirit prompted my reaching toward them. I felt I needed to write, not to try to change them but to keep a connection and to share my interest in them. For me to stay spiritually healthy my inner voice urged me to write these letters.

Advanced Journal Insert, February 6, 1999

Today George Alexenko, now 85, is ill and in a Goshen nursing home. My regular visits with him have been interesting and rewarding. Yesterday George and I reviewed our diminishing differences and our common faith commitments. George talks about death and asked if I would come to his memorial. As I left him to go to the parking lot, he turned on his flashlight and used it to wave farewell from his window.

It was a grace-filled moment!
George tested me at times, even as I tested him. George enlarged my human understandings, increased my compassion and enriched my faith. I thank God for George, my brother in Christ. I thank God for RECONCILING GRACE and for its continuing work among us.

December 27, 1985

Recently I read an interesting and critical analysis of Irish life and culture. The book On Bended Knee *is written by Rosita Sweetman. The following quotes are from her book:*

> *"In Ireland there are two acceptable reactions to a crisis. The first is to get on your knees and pray to God. The second is to go down on one knee, lift a gun and try to shoot the head off of your opponent."*

> *"Violence is part and parcel of the Irish national psyche. There's the collective violence of the new bourgeoisie perpetrated on the poor. There's the psychological violence perpetrated by the Church on everybody all the time. Then there's the violence of the North and that is a violence everyone recognizes."*

> *"In the South of Ireland we eat more calories per head, per day than any other race in the world (eat includes drink; in fact, apart from food we spend more on drink than any other item. The pub is the center of Irish life. Priests like to think the church is, but the church is a place where men go between pubs and women go between babies. In N. Ireland five percent of the people own 47 percent of the wealth, and in S. Ireland five percent own 75 percent of the wealth."*

Interesting, but I have some questions about the above since the author does not give adequate supporting evidence for her projections.

Dublin, December 29, 1985

Late this afternoon I had a stimulating two hours with Briefine Walker. He is doing a study on the just war theory in the context of Northern Ireland. He feels the IRA is modifying the theory and is using it to rationalize their violence. Walker thinks Mennonites can help place the content of Christian pacifism on the Catholic/Protestant agenda, no small task. He is seriously interested in changing the meaning of pacifism from a passive, do nothing state to active, transforming nonviolent action. This aspect Walker feels has received scant attention in Ireland.

Dublin, January 13, 1986

I don't quite know what has happened since last writing. Our days are numbered here. I begin to feel some leaving pressure! Martin Tierney, director of internal communications for the Catholic Church, was here for lunch and talk today. He has written a book on cults. At an earlier time he thought Mennonites might be in that category. Mike (Guarde) helped clarify that question. Today Tierney is a strong supporter of Mike's educational and counseling work with those caught in cults and certain new religious movements. Tierney thinks there is a place for Mennonites in the Irish religious setting.

Dublin, January 15, 1986

Hurrah. Winnie and I finished our 40-page report today! The report gives statistical data, interpretive comments, summary of findings and questions for further study coming out of interviews we had with members of the Dublin Mennonite community, a sampling of active Christians in the Dublin area and a similar group from North Ireland. There were suggestions for strengthened pastoral care and improved decision-making for the Dublin community. In addition, there was affirmation for a continuing Mennonite presence in the Republic and for a Mennonite peace and mediation witness in the North that would

Irish Blessing

May the road rise to meet you,
May the wind be always at your back,
May the sun shine warm upon your face,
The rain fall soft upon your fields.
And, until we meet again,
May the Lord God hold you
In the hollow of His hand.

be linked to and supportive of Irish efforts. The report needs much
discussion and processing by the Dublin Community and other groups.
We had good cooperation. The interviewing was personally stimulating
and enriching. The participation by so many thoughtful and busy
people is a tribute to the witness and the relationships built up by the
Dublin Community these past five years. The sponsoring agencies owe
a great debt to those who participated in the study.

Dublin, January 16, 1986

Linda picked us up at 9:15 to take us shopping. Our first stop was
Dublin Woolens where Winnie and I were each given beautiful Arian
sweaters as a thank you for our presence here the past five months. At
first I had a conscience problem about the cost but overcame it when
Linda insisted it was the will of the community!

Dublin, January 18, 1986

The community had a gracious farewell for us last evening. Peter sang
Irish songs. There were short farewell speeches. Greta shared a
beautiful cake. Winnie and I modeled our sweaters. We learned to
love, respect and appreciate each member of the community and their
special gifts and concerns, including the gifts the children brought to
the community. We feel a strong bond to these sisters and brothers and
to their vision. We have been enriched by their faith, struggles and
commitment and take their hopes with us and promise our support
and prayers. We also leave part of ourselves in this place. May God's
enabling grace flow into and guide this witness. Thank you, God, for
this experience.

Dublin, January 20, 1986

This morning I changed my motivation for jogging. I resolved to jog for
the pure pleasure of the experience. Jogging is a time to look up and

around and to drink in my surroundings. Scenes, people, situations are now coming to life in a new way. I decided to take it easier on the inclines and to stop for an occasional breather. These provide recovery moments, time to enjoy a special scene and to let my imagination run. Today I saw a flock of ducks looking for food in the canal. A hundred meters away 10 lovely white swans looked very pleased with themselves. I met many people walking themselves and their dogs, both species coming in all shapes and sizes. I discovered the leaves and shrubs were putting on an impressive show, displaying a rich and lovely panorama of colors.

Studying facial expressions was interesting and reflected a wide range. There were friendly faces, cheerful smiles and Irish greetings. Some faces were lined with age, experience, serenity, hope and integrity. Other faces were marked with anxiety, pain, despair, loneliness and hostility. My inner voice affirms the validity of my change in motivation. A final reflection–joggers and MCCers have some common goals. Both are interested in God's creation and human development. Why not try jogging?

MCC Akron, September 27, 1986

The past eight months have passed rapidly. Besides normal MCC Peace Section work we were asked to review Ron Sider's Mennonite World Conference peace corps proposal. Considerable time and energy are being invested in getting responses to his idea of having a considerable number of nonviolent peacemakers that would be trained to intervene in violent situations by being nonviolent buffers between warring sides. I am also completing a brochure titled "The Peacemaking Commitment Of The Mennonite Central Committee."

Our leaving date is coming up soon. I have been asked to give a chapel on my spiritual journal with emphasis on the peace and justice dimension. I read the request to mean this: explain who you are and why. Interesting and demanding! These three years have been growth years for me. My faith in and support of MCC's mission have been affirmed and expanded. Leaving this active dedicated faith community is not easy.

A Prayer for Mennonite Central Committee

Loving God, on this special day of remembering, we thank you for bringing into being the Mennonite Central Committee. We thank you for calling the representatives of Mennonite relief agencies together in Elkhart on July 27, 1920, for placing a vision in their heads and for igniting a fire in their hearts. Today we celebrate your wondrous work in and through MCC.

Loving God, you called thousands to share bread and water "in the name and spirit of Christ." You called thousands and thousands into meat canning, quilting, self-help, relief sales, kit making, and many other love-in-action projects. You touched millions in your reconciling and healing ministries through MCC.

Loving God, for calling us to your ministry to the hungry, the oppressed and the broken, we thank you. For tenderizing our hearts, for challenging our attitudes and values, for enlarging our vision and our understanding of your work in the world, we thank you. And especially we thank you for teaching us so much through your followers and others in many lands.

Loving God, keep us responsive to the needs in this congregation, this community and across the world. Let the voices of the poor, the oppressed, and all who suffer pain and prejudice disturb us. Keep us humble. Keep us from weariness. Renew and restore our souls. We thank you for blessing and guiding MCC these past 75 years and for making MCC an expression of our faith and an agent for peace and justice. In this day of massive greed, exploding violence and unlimited opportunities use each one of us to help MCC in its reconciling ministries in the world. We pray in the name of Jesus–Savior, Lord and Prince of Peace. Amen.

> –College Mennonite Church celebration of MCC's 75th anniversary, September 24, 1995

Seniors for Peace, 1986+

Chapter Fifteen

Remembering the human costs of war, dreaming of a world without war and serious commitment to work for such a world are essential in peacemaking. In December 1986 representatives from different Mennonite groups gathered in Chicago to discuss Ron Sider's nonviolent intervention peacemaking proposal and the need for a revitalized peace witness. Interest was strong. The discussion continued in a car en route to Goshen.

Everyone agreed on the need and opportunity but someone asked where would the peacemakers come from. Greater involvement of seniors was suggested as a way to increase resources. I shared the idea with our K-group, who agreed that "senior power" could be useful in teaching peace and justice to children and youth as well as for witnessing to the power of God's love in reconciling human beings to each other and in reducing violence and war in the world. I tested the idea further with older friends and church leaders. There was strong affirmation.

Seniors for Peace

Faith Requires Expression. Righteousness and reconciliation are the Christian's vocation. God wants you to follow the Prince of Peace. No 10 percent discount in peace witnessing for seniors. You are needed and you count, and the rewards are great.

The Biblical Mandate. "All this is from God, who through Christ reconciled us to Himself and gave us the ministry of reconciliation." II Corinthians 5:18.

The December 1986 Peace Conference. Representatives of four Mennonite groups met in Chicago to review the Christian Peacemaker Team proposal and peace and justice needs and opportunities. The conference concluded that:

> We believe the mandate to proclaim the Gospel of repentance, salvation and reconciliation includes a strengthened Biblical peace witness.
>
> We believe that faithfulness to what Jesus taught and modeled calls us to more active peacemaking.
>
> We believe a renewed commitment to the Gospel of peace calls us to new forms of public witness, which may include non-violent direct action.
>
> We believe the establishment of Christian Peacemaker Teams is an important new dimension for our on-going peace and justice ministries.

Seniors and this Call. Peace education and witness is the vocation of all–not just draft-age youth. How do seniors fit into this effort? What range of witness opportunities will encourage and challenge seniors to greater involvement? How can the experiences, understandings and skills of older people be used in building shalom communities?

Why "Seniors for Peace" Now? Because

> **The biblical mandate demands a response.**
>
> **The threat of nuclear and conventional wars and the growing violence everywhere cry out for reconciliation efforts.**
> **Seniors want their children and their grandchildren to have a future.**

For the sake of their spiritual health, seniors need and want to be involved in doing something constructive for peace, outreach and justice.

The "Seniors for Peace" Vision. The dream calls for small, congregational and community-based groups who are committed to following Christ's way of reconciliation and nonviolence. They meet regularly to study the word, pray, share and support each other. They help each other discern God's will for each individual and for the group in various forms of peace witnessing.

What Might Seniors Do? There are many ways to witness to Christ's righteousness and reconciliation. Individuals and groups are encouraged to select those patterns of witness which are right for them.

Our K-group, Evelyn and Carl Kreider, Ethel and the late Roy Umble, and Winifred and I became the Seniors For Peace Coordinating Committee. Our group's focus has been two-fold. We encouraged seniors to get more involved in peace and justice witness. We also responded to many local, national and international peace and justice issues through prayer, discernment, letters and other acts of affirmation and protest. Through these actions, we hoped to maintain a peace and justice presence in all aspects of our lives. To start a SFP group, peace proponents can bring together a few interested persons to share tea, peace stories, and concerns. Together they discern, pray and try to begin reducing violence and increasing love, peace and justice everywhere. Another pattern has developed in Goshen, where monthly meetings inform seniors on issues with encouragement for them to respond.

A Response to the INF Treaty, 1987

Early afternoon December 8, 1987, General Secretary Mikhail Gorbachev and President Ronald Reagan signed the INF treaty eliminating all intermediate-range nuclear missiles. The two leaders talked

> *of a new outlook, a new spirit and the possibilities of a new world as the cameras recorded and the reporters described and analyzed this potentially historic event.*
>
> *We planted a peace tree to celebrate this new beginning. A few days later several of our friends joined us to dedicate the tree and ourselves to Christ's continuing ministry of reconciliation that comes to all who follow Him. We planted our tree in remembrance of God's reconciling grace and action in the world and in hope-hope that the tree will grow and remind us of our task and hope that the INF treaty will grow and move us toward the day when all nations "shall beat their swords into plowshares, and their spears into pruning hooks." Isaiah 2:4*

What else have seniors done? An early project initiated by the Ontario Seniors for Peace was selling jute shopping bags from Bangladesh. Some seniors protest military spending by withholding the military portion of their income taxes and contribute it to a peace fund. A Canadian couple turned their home into a "House of Intercession" from which they work for peace and justice. Some work with prisoners in local jails, protest the death penalty and work for reform in the judicial system. Others organize inter-generational peace conversations and practice hospitality to the lonely, alienated or those holding opposing views. Still other seniors write protest and support letters to political and religious leaders, to editors, to the oppressed and to those designated as enemies. Below is one such exchange with children's author, Dr. Seuss (the late Theodor Geisel, 1904-1991).

Exchange of Letters with Dr. Seuss

> *Dear Dr. Seuss:*
>
> *Please accept my belated best wishes for your birthday. I am grateful for your 44 books for children. What a wonderful contribution you have made!*

I've been deeply impressed by your Butter Battle Book. The story and the illustrations combine to make this the most lucid and powerful description of human behavior in our current frightful condition that I have ever seen. And I have looked at many books since I am a retired professor of peace studies. I do not give this endorsement lightly. I recently sent a copy of your book to a peace education center in Belfast after a visit to that agonizing city. It applies to the two communities in Northern Ireland as it does to thousands of other settings. It should be required reading for all world leaders, including lawmakers. The book should be in every school across the world in the needed translations.

I wish you energy, wisdom and humor for your continued story telling.

Peace, joy and hope,

Atlee Beechy
Consultant, Mennonite Central Committee Peace Section

Response from Dr. Seuss, April 1986

Dear Atlee Beechy,

Thank you for your very warm and friendly letter of April 10. At a time when so much of the world seems intent on blowing itself up, it was a comforting and encouraging experience to read the commendations you so generously sent me.

With kindest regards and all best wishes.

Dr. Seuss
Theodor S. Geisel

Seniors are concerned about environmental issues, the land mine evil, nuclear proliferation, the Comprehensive Test Ban Treaty, and human rights violations as carried out in

I Beat a Drum for Peace

Everyone beats a drum.

I beat a drum for peace and righteousness.

I beat a drum for God's call for shalom.

I beat a drum for Christ's reconciling death on the cross, His redeeming resurrection, His call to share "in the ministry of reconciliation."

I beat a drum for Christ's gentle and indestructible Spirit that cleanses, comforts, confronts and nudges.

I beat a drum for Christian martyrs whose lives and deaths make a powerful witness for shalom and conscience.

I beat a drum for those who work for healing and reconciliation in homes, classrooms, prisons, businesses, mediation centers, courts, hospitals, factories, offices, farms, churches and in many other settings.

I beat a drum for parents and teachers who model and teach their children the way of peace.

I beat a drum for children, youth, adults and middle-agers who commit themselves to the demands, excitement and frustrations of peacemaking.

I beat a drum for seniors who are active peacemakers using their hearts, minds, experiences and skills in peace witnessing.

I challenge everyone to beat a drum for peace!

racism, sexism and economic exploitation. Goshen Seniors for Peace protested military games and gun shows at our county fair and brought about a change in policy. Seniors helped to sponsor monthly peace forums. During the Persian Gulf war they prepared black armbands for distribution to members of the congregation and students who wished to wear them as symbols of mourning for all who suffered because of the war. SFP helped establish College Mennonite Church Peace Center and give strong support for strengthening peace witness, education and research at Goshen College. These are a few examples of what seniors are doing. Needs and opportunities continue to call us.

What has my 12-year involvement in Seniors for Peace meant to me? The years have been exciting, spiritually enriching, demanding and satisfying. God's unrationed grace and God's call to reconciling ministry, prayer, connectedness, and mutual accountability continue to provide motivation and meaning to my soul and confirm that peacemaking is my vocation!

Peacemaking: an Ongoing Response, 1990s

Chapter Sixteen

Conflict continues to erupt among individuals, ethnic and religious groups, and nations. The Persian Gulf war, using psychological techniques and modern technology, produced a high-powered propaganda machine that misled many. Later in the decade, our intervention in Kosovo was well intentioned, but brought misery to many. War always brings pain, and requires our response.

October 11, 1990, The Gulf War

The winds of war are blowing. In a few short months the world has moved from "peace is breaking out" to the brink of war. The lines are drawn in the sand, and the war drums are beating. Threats and counter-threats become more strident, The guns, tanks, missiles, bombs, ships and planes are poised. A war is waiting to happen.

How can this be? Psychological warfare by both sides is in high gear. Distorted facts and images are essential parts of this process. Words that generate hate and fear become weapons. Nations have egos. They need and create new enemies. Truth is becoming a casualty. National self-interests and greed for oil, land, water, power, status are hidden behind high-sounding, self-righteous, moral pronouncements. God or Allah will give us the victory. History is selectively used or ignored. We project the best possible face on ourselves and the worst, demonized face on our new enemy. The making of the enemy is a pre-condition for war. This

A Sheep's Prayer

*Dear Shepherd Jesus
This sheep has a problem.
The time is 3:56 a.m.,
My eyes stay open and my mind flips
And races across the world.
Still my heart and my thoughts. Quiet my
Spirit and lead me into the paths of sleep.
Amen.*

formula is as old as war itself. Mennonites are not immune to this heavy barrage of war propaganda. What is new today is the availability of modern communication technology and more sophisticated psychological techniques to do the propagandizing.

Psychological warfare is a major ingredient in generating the war climate and in carrying out the killing. Mark Twain undresses psychological warfare for what it is in The Mysterious Stranger, *published after his death in 1905. John Foster Dulles, the late U.S. Secretary of State in the 1950s, explains the psychological build-up for war in these words, "In order to bring a nation to support the burdens of maintaining great military establishments, it is necessary to create an emotional climate akin to war psychology. There must be the portrayal of an external menace. This involves the development to a high degree of the nation hero, the nation villain and the arousing of the population to a sense of sacrifice. Once these exist, we have gone a long way on the path to war." The Persian Gulf war has these characteristics. Wake-up time is here!*

A Plea to President George Bush and President Saddam Hussein, January 4, 1991

You both are religious men. In the name of the God you profess to follow, PLEASE DO NOT GO TO WAR!

You are both family men. In the name of your children and grandchildren and the millions more who would be affected, PLEASE DO NOT GO TO WAR!

You both say you do not want to go to war and want a peaceful resolution. In the name of reason, common sense and humanity, seriously pursue your stated intent and PLEASE DO NOT GO TO WAR.

You both talk about a new world order that corrects long standing injustices. In the name of hope for that new world order and new ways

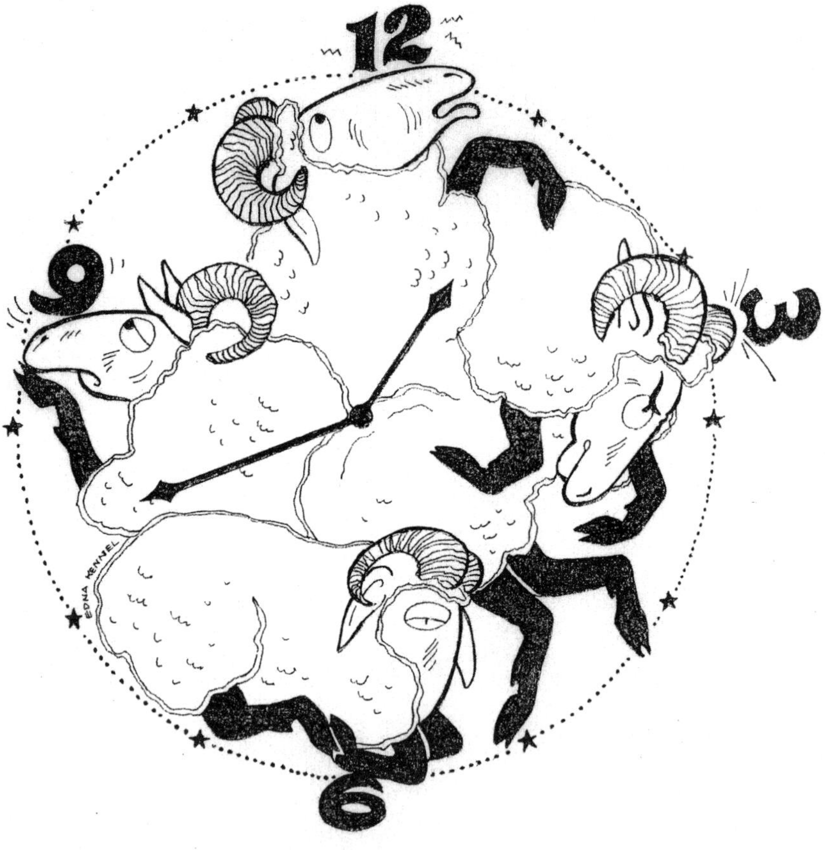
12
9
3
6
EDNA KENNEL

to settle conflicts, PLEASE DO NOT GO TO WAR!

You both have threatened each other, set deadlines and are playing the brinkmanship game and now have little space and time for the United Nations peacemaking process to work. In the name of preventing another holocaust and in the name of sanity, PLEASE DO NOT GO TO WAR!

You both are key players in this crisis in history and what you do in these next weeks will determine the way the world goes and how history judges. In the name of history and your place in it PLEASE DO NOT GO TO WAR.

Millions of people in Iraq, the United States and in many other countries desperately want peace and are daily praying for peace. The well known military leader and statesman, Dwight D. Eisenhower, late in his life said, " I like to believe that people in the long run are going to do more to promote peace than are governments. Indeed, I think that people want peace so much that one of these days governments had better get out of their way and let them have it."

*Respectfully yours,
Professor Emeritus Atlee Beechy and Winifred Beechy*

No, this letter did not change the course of history, but there are times when we must write or speak because our inner voices demand it.

The call for peace in the Persian Gulf war came with power and conviction from the pulpit at College Mennonite Church. Sunday school discussions and special forums informed and opened channels for sharing and support. Middle and high school students from the congregation gave clear and courageous peace witness in their schools. The Goshen College Peace Studies Program helped educate the student body and the community about the issues. Seniors for Peace organized weekly prayer gatherings before and during the Gulf war. SFP made

Seek Peace and Pursue It
March 2, 1991

The killing has stopped. Thank God.

Victory has been declared.

What has been won?

I think of 41 days of air war, of 100,000 sorties and the death and destruction that dropped down from the sky, and I weep.

I think of 100 hours of ground war killing and destruction, of burning oil wells and of unexploded mines, and I weep.

I think of massive war expenditures, the stealing from the sick, the homeless and millions of children dying for want of food, medicine and I weep.

I think of my tax dollars that helped buy this sophisticated military machine that kills so impersonally and efficiently, and I weep.

I think of oil and personal and corporate greed and American affluence and many, many thousands of Iraqi civilian causalities, and I weep.

I think of Shalom, the new community where "righteousness and peace embrace," love and the well-being of all are sought, and I hope and pray!

Victory has been declared.

Where is the peace?

available black armbands to interested members and students. Many wore these symbols of mourning for all who died as a protest against the war until the war ended.

Sunday, December 1, 1996

A Prayer for the People of Central Africa

> God of all humanity, we lift up to you and to ourselves the suffering and burdens of the world. Thank you for those who inform us and disturb us. Let the cries of children pierce our hearts. Today we lift up to your compassionate and healing grace the refugees on the roads and in the camps in Zaire, Burundi and Rwanda, as they search for their families, for sustenance, for home and for peace. We weep for the homeless, the hungry, the thirsty, the tired, the lonely, the sick, the grieving, the fearful and the despairing. Move us beyond our tears to compassionate action.
>
> God, continue to call your followers to minister to the suffering. Work in the hearts of church and political leaders so that genuine peace and healing may come. Let hate be transformed into love. Disturb our consciences and the consciences of the church and world so that food and medicine may flow freely into this tragedy. Forgive our indifference and slow response. Awaken our compassion. Open our eyes, our hearts and our moneybags so that others may live. Let our sharing be generous and cheerful. Strengthen the burned-out workers. Give us vision and commitment for the long-term hope and peace-building task in Central Africa. Amen.

April 8, 1999

A Prayer for the People of Serbia and Kosovo

> God, we lift up to you and to ourselves the suffering,
> dislocation, killing and deeply-etched fear and hate
> that fuel the madness of this war.
> God, we weep and we mourn with you
> for all who are caught in this tragedy.
> We hear the cries of children, mothers and the old
> as the bombs, missiles and guns destroy and kill.
> Keep our hearts tender and open to the pain.
> God, may your amazing and reconciling grace
> Penetrate this conflict.
> May your grace change the hearts of Milosevic,
> Clinton and other political and religious leaders.
> Let them seek peace and pursue it
> in creative, non-killing ways.
> Break open and transform the long-standing
> fear and hate into trust and hope.
> God, there are many other arenas of violence;
> United States, Iraq, Sudan, Indonesia, Middle East, Burma, Ireland,
> Central Africa and in our own hearts.
> God, we praise you for your work in the world
> and for calling us into your ministry of reconciliation.
> Deliver us from weariness,
> Renew our hearts and our commitments,
> Keep us faithful in praying and working for peace.
> Amen.

Violence and Nonviolence Class, May 1981

Reflections on Memorial Day

> I am opposed to all war.
> The Gospel says no to war.
> My humanity says no to war.
> My mind says no to war,
> My sense of justice says no to war.
> My heart says no to war.
>
> I am for peace.
> The Gospel says yes to peace.
> My humanity says yes to peace.
> My mind says yes to peace.
> My sense of justice says yes to peace.
> My heart says yes to peace.
> What difference will it make
> If the eleven of us say
> No to war and yes to peace?
> Time and our children will answer!

Transitions: Places and People, 1996+

Chapter Seventeen

For 40 years we called 1916 Woodward Place home. In 1956 Winnie planned the living spaces and transformed the plans into a lively and renewing home base. The children were picked up early each day by school bus and returned after the school day. The joy and pain of learning were shared at meal time. We watched College Woods emerge from a field of weeds into a beautiful arboretum. In this house we spent many joyful hours with close friends–the Umbles, the Massanaris, the Kreiders, the Kauffmans, the Gingerichs, the Hershbergers and others. Children were important in the bonding of the families. We watched our children grow and mature. In this house our three daughters dressed for their weddings and moved into the next stage of their lives.

Thoughts on the Night Before Leaving 1916 Woodward Place

In August 1956 Winnie and I, with daughters Karen, Judith and Susan, moved with joy and anticipation into our first minimally owned home.

Roots went down, found nourishment and treasured memories accumulated.

Love for this place, the beautiful neighbors and the environs deepened.

My Flowering Crab

It is May after a long, depressing Indiana winter.
My soul is dry, tired and reaches for renewal.
My flowering crab hears my cry and dresses up in brilliant pink.
My soul and heart are quickly restored.
My animal friends had dreary and cold days too.
Their bodies and hearts are dry and hungry.
They gather in my flowering crab to suck energy juice.
Their bodies and hearts are quickly restored.
They decorate my tree with color and song.

My animal friends–
      a gray squirrel,
      a black squirrel,
      a chipmunk,
      a humming bird and
      a cardinal–
Gather this sunny afternoon to enjoy their banquet
And together celebrate the long-awaited coming of Spring!

More than being a physical structure, this place became our emotional and spiritual home.

Here the juices flowed and we learned to know and love and sometimes hurt each other.

Wife, daughters, and granddaughters, grandsons and in-laws taught me much about life, love, liberation and hope.

In spite of commitment to simple living our 40-year material accumulation has been considerable even without attic or basement.

Downsizing by sharing our possessions with MCC, Salvation Army, and Goodwill was a good experience.

Our beloved books went to AAUW, to Books Abroad, to peace centers and to friends.

These moments alone on the back porch bring back many precious memories.

The memories and the night voices—the moon and stars, the birds, the crickets, and the tower chimes—speak of peace and a great Creator.

The in-season fragrances come to me with comforting support as my heart weeps!

Tomorrow we leave this "palace" with considerable pain and sense of loss.

Our grief is tempered by knowing that Marty and Ron will lovingly occupy this place.

I thank God for guiding and blessing our lives during our 40 wonderful years here.

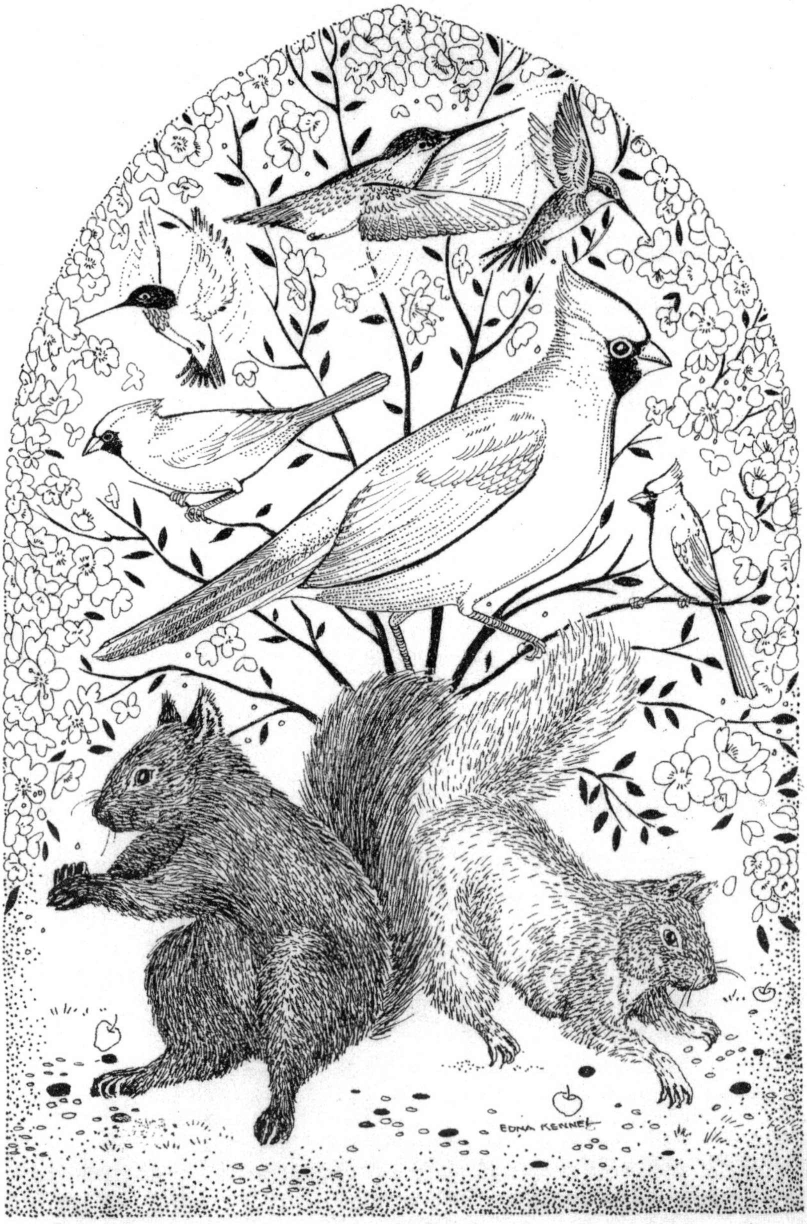
EDNA KENNEL

I pray that God's Spirit will continue to grace this house and those who occupy it.

I thank God for the many who shared life in this house, for they greatly enriched our lives.

I know God's grace will accompany us as we soon move to 1524 Dogwood Court.

Good-bye dear house and thanks for the memories.

All of our children gathered to say goodbye to the house. Karen, our eldest daughter, created a special "House Farewell" litany for this occasion. Each family member carried a candle as we moved from room to room sharing stories and important events that had occurred in that room. Appropriate scriptures were read, with different family members responding with prayers

As Winnie read the final antiphon, we all joined in:

Winnie:	*Oh heavenly Father, of whom the whole family in heaven and earth is named, be present in this house, that all who live here, being kindly affectioned one to another, may find it a haven of blessing and of peace, through Jesus Christ our Lord. Amen.*
Leader:	*Let us bless the Lord.*
Family:	*Thanks be to God.*
People:	*The almighty and merciful Lord, the Father, the Son and the Holy Spirit, bless us and keep us. Amen*

One Snap Dragon Speaks to Me
December 15, 1998, Goshen, Indiana

Where have all the flowers gone?
In spite of frost and cold winds, you cheerfully
insist on displaying your six beautiful blooms.
You stand alone with quiet dignity, grace and power.
The rest of the flowers bowed to December's demands.
Each day you welcome all who find you.
I look, listen, absorb and my heart is warmed.
Your smile, your beauty and your example
awaken courage, hope and love.

September 17, 1998

Good-bye for Now
(Written upon the death of long-time friend Dwight Yoder)

> I rejoice in memories of what was—
> a productive life, a gentle spirit, a goodly heritage.
> I recognize and accept the painful disintegration of your mind and body.
> But found in the flashes of our connections,
> the mystery of God's unrationed grace.
> Let us remember and give thanks. . . .
> Peace and grace until we meet again.

Journal Entry October 30, 1999

> Today George (Alexanko) was sleeping when I arrived. He woke up but seemed a little groggy. He didn't want me to leave. He became very warm, held on to my hands and kissed them several times. On leaving he wanted me to come by his window again so we could say good-bye. He waved his lighted flashlight as I drove away. I thank God for George and for love, making us friends in spite of some serious differences. We accept each other as brothers in Christ.

Journal Entry December 26, 1999

> Today I asked George if he liked chocolate and if he is allowed to eat it. His answer, "yes" to both questions. I gave him two Hershey kisses. His face lit up and he immediately ate one. We talked about God, the break-up of communism in Russia, the current corruption and suffering among the people and the recent election. I offered to read the Luke 2 Christmas story or the 23rd Psalm. Which would he like me to read? "Both," he replied. We ended on a deep spiritual note wishing each other God's blessing and grace.

My Peace Pond
July 7, 1998

My heart needs quieting and refilling.
Thank You God for this peace-generating place!

Here I find "quiet waters,"
a symphony of color,
graceful ducks and their children,
a family of eloquent swans,
birds and frogs competing in song,
gentle breezes cooling my brow,
friendly sun announcing dawn,
Your creation speaks peace to me.

But there is another world out there,
a world of hate and fear,
of hunger and greed,
of beatings and killings,
of knives and guns,
of inner and outer wars.
Empower me to engage this second world!

Visions of the Future, 2000

Chapter Eighteen

"The Greatest of These is Love"

I dream of a world in which love comes to every person on this planet and in which each individual becomes an active channel of sharing love with others. Impossible? God's unrationed, transforming grace and love are wonderful resources to work at this challenge!

I believe love is the heart of the faith experience and of conflict transformation and peacemaking. Experiencing and responding to God's love is central in the biblical story of reconciliation. We become reconciled to God, each other and ourselves through accepting and responding to God's agape love and grace. This experience and love from family and others calls me into my vocation – joyfully working in Christ's ministry of reconciliation.

What is love? Matthew 5 and Luke 4:18 - 19 tell me what love is about. Paul's words in I Corinthians 13 have been speaking to me since I memorized them when I was in my teens.

> *If I could speak in any language in heaven or on earth but didn't love others, I would only be making meaningless noise like a loud gong or a clanging cymbal. If I had the gift of prophecy, and I knew all the mysteries of the future and knew everything about everything but didn't love others, what good would I be? And if I had the gift of faith so*

that I could speak to a mountain and make it move, without love I would be no good to anybody. If I gave everything I have to the poor and even sacrificed my body, I could boast about it; but if I didn't love others, I would be of no value whatsoever.

Love is patient and kind. Love is not jealous or boastful or proud or rude. Love does not demand its own way. Love is not irritable, and it keeps no record of when it has been wronged. It is never glad about injustice but rejoices when the truth wins out. Love never gives up, never loses faith, is always hopeful, and endures through every circumstance. . . .

There are three things that will endure – faith, hope and love – and the greatest of these is love. (I Corinthians 13:1-7, 13)

Love – loving and being loved – are very important for spiritual and emotional health in today's individualistic, materialistic, fragmented and violent world. Love is no longer the concern only of poets, romantics, novelists, philosophers, movie directors and religious leaders. Today social scientists, social workers, reformers, counselors, community organizers, medical personnel, ministers and teachers recognize that love plays a critical role in healthy human development as well as being a great healing power for those imprisoned in anxiety, guilt and hate. Montagu points out the importance of love when he says, "To live as if to live and love were one is not a new recommendation; what is new is that the meaning of love should have been rediscovered in the twentieth century by scientific means." Victor Frankl states, "Love is the only way to grasp another human being in the innermost core of his personality. No one can become fully aware of the very essence of another human being unless he loves him." Maslow concludes that "we must understand love; we must be able to teach it, to create it, to predict it or else the world is lost to hostility and suspicion." Emily Balch presents the challenge in these words: "We have a long way to go. So let us hasten along the road, the roads of human tenderness and generosity. Groping we may find one another's hand in the dark." Love is the key to survival with meaning.

Human beings are created to be loved and to love. This idea is an important thesis in my 1958 dissertation in which I have a 23-page chapter on the impact of love on personality. We learn most about love through experiencing it and sharing it. If we are to be free to love and be loved, we must improve the quality of the physical, spiritual and emotional space in which we live. The ultimate test of our peace and justice witness is reducing fear, hate and violence and increasing trust, hope and love.

Most religions of the world have beautiful rhetoric about love, but a careful evaluation of the world's condition suggests we have a great surplus of hate and violence and a huge shortage of love and trust. If religions would live out what they profess about love, they would change the world. Love is not soft and flabby nor outdated. Love is the most powerful force for personal and systemic change. In 1883 Henry Drummond called love the greatest force in the world. Sorokin studied the effects of love on individuals and society. His research supports Drummond's thesis. We know that love cells radically committed to the Jesus way of nonviolent love are making a difference. Let God's love and grace feed our souls, energize our minds, spirits, and bodies, and ignite joy for engaging in Christ's unfinished ministry of reconciliation!

My Dream for the Future: Goshen College, the Mennonite Church and the World

I have been greatly enriched and inspired by a growing family of active, dedicated peacemakers around the world. Bishop Dom Helder Camara until his death in 1999 worked on peace and justice issues in Brazil for many years. Speaking of the future, he observed, "There are people who are equipped with the power of love and justice and they can be likened to nuclear energy locked for millions of years in the smallest atoms waiting to be released."

I believe that as these love atoms connect with each other, they will explode and release their energy into building a more peaceful and just world. This is what happened to my friends, a Muslim and his Catholic wife. They are both professors in Bangkok universities, he a teacher of political science and she a specialist in Buddhism. Both discovered nonviolence, and they have become activists in the world peace movement. He believes the Qur'an teaches nonviolence. She finds the same to be true of Buddhism. They make a powerful team. I think of the Israeli soldier I met in Jerusalem who was waiting to get out of the military so that he could follow his conscience and work for peace openly, of a sixth grader who is very active in school mediation, of the high school student who made a clear witness against the Persian Gulf war mania, of a 19-year-old Colombian who has spent time in prison because he is refusing to become part of the military, of a retired senior couple in Manitoba who spend full time in peace and justice work and who have made their home "a house of peace," of a Christian Peacemaker team helping to shut down a crack house in Washington and of an Mennonite Central Committee couple who see their primary objective in a violent African country as being the reconciling presence. The development in MCC of International Conciliation Service is exciting. I am encouraged when 15 retired U.S. generals ask the President to stop the use of land mines, and a high school junior wins a United Nation's contest with a brilliant essay on this same topic, though much work still remains to be done on this issue. George E. Kennan, retired American statesman and expert on Russian affairs, says in his recently released book of memoirs, " But I find myself now, and only very recently, in my older years, coming for the first time to the conclusion that it is not enough even to eliminate nuclear weapons from the national arsenals, that the day has passed when war itself in any form, conventional or otherwise is permissible." Yes, let us not lose heart. The winds of peace are blowing.

Peacemaking also is what "Culture for Service" is all about – healing, caring for and witnessing to the world of the

Jesus nonviolent way, reducing violence, and building peace-generating individuals and communities. I dream of a day when all Goshen College graduates move into the world with clear commitments and the needed understandings and skills to work for peace and justice in whatever daily work they are doing. I dream that resources for strengthening peace, justice and conflict studies will become available, including funding for some type of peace institute. In the peacemaking vocation I have found opportunity to use all of my capacity to love, my creativity, intelligence, patience, courage and sense of humor! I believe God has opened unlimited domestic and international peace and justice opportunities and urgently calls us to be the reconciling presence and action wherever there is pain and violence.

If the church is to have credibility in its peace and justice witness, it must be spiritually healthy and consistently live and teach Christ's reconciling message. This means, I believe, that again and again we must face, confess, repent, forgive and deal with our discriminatory attitudes and behaviors, our inner civil wars, our destructive conflicts with each other and our violent thoughts, words and actions. We are to be open and accountable to each other. For this to happen God's amazing and healing grace needs to penetrate our total being. Transformation and renewal are essential for our spiritual health and for the integrity of our peace and justice witness.

Occasionally, I find my peace and justice journey frustrating and overwhelming. There are times when I need to stop running and check if I am on the right highway and see if my priorities are in line with my core beliefs and values. I also need to check if my running speed is legal, humane and Christian. Ninety-five percent of the time I am finding the journey exciting, instructive, enriching, and wonderfully satisfying. I draw vision and energy from God, the scriptures, and from students, the middle-aged and seniors in my faith community. Much inspiration and great spiritual energy flow into my heart from those I meet on my peace journey. I encourage you to make the reconciling ministry your primary vocation.

Confessions of a Peacemaker

O God of peace,
  wars go on inside my heart
      between good and evil,
      hope and despair,
      love and hatred.
Disarm my heart from the sin that binds it.

Lord have mercy on me.
I confess that I become hardened
to the cries of the poor.
I keep silent when I should
speak up for peace and justice.

Lord have mercy on me.
I confess being too glum and self-righteous,
trying to carry too much on my back,
forgetting that God and others also care.
Increase my faith and risk-taking.
Help me walk in cheerful compassion.

Lord, I confess that I hold on
to infecting bitterness.
I preach peace but am afraid
to face the violence in me.
I impose rather than elicit.

I contribute to tensions and conflict.
I am slow to seek or extend forgiveness.
I am implicated in evil systems that
bind and oppress – war,
racism, sexism.
I confuse my needs and wants,
I eat from full tables while others
starve.
I use pious words and flimsy excuses
for not getting involved in the world's pain.

Lord have mercy on me.
"Wash me thoroughly from my iniquity and
cleanse me from my sin. Create in me a
clean heart, O God, and put a new and
right spirit within me. "
Amen

1988

I close with a story that comes out of the agony of the Middle East:

A respected teacher asked his students, when does the night end and the day is on its way back?

"Could it be," asked one student, "when you can see an animal in the distance and tell if it is a sheep or a dog?"

"No," answered the teacher.

"Could it be," asked another student, "when you look at a tree in the distance and tell if it is a fig tree or an olive tree?"

"No" answered the teacher.

"Well, then when is it?" his students demanded.

"It is when you look on the face of any woman or man or child from any nation, clan or race in the world and see that she or he is your sister or brother. Because if you cannot do that, then no matter what time it is, it is still night."

"Seek peace and pursue it" until the day comes!

The End of the Journey

Looking back on my journey has led me to write this memoir. The review reminds me of the importance of grace, love, memories, roots, dreams and relationships in bringing degrees of hell or heaven into the interpersonal fabric of life and also in generating wars and in building peace. Memories and dreams may imprison, instruct, liberate or inspire. Relationships may carry healing trust and love or destructive hate and fear. They determine the nature and quality of life in the family, community and world.

I cannot see the end of my journey, though my body and mind give me signals as to where I am in my journey. In February 2000 I was diagnosed as having Paget's disease, a rare form of skin cancer. After 25 radiation treatments I am now pretty well recovered from the effects of radiation. A few days ago Doctor Richard called to say that the biopsy of a small lump on my back indicated that cancer was present. Today I had a CAT scan to see if the cancer is spreading. The ending of my journey and the beginning of my new life are not for me to see at this time. I choose to face reality but not to focus on what is or might be but to see each day as a gift of God and to draw on wonderful memories of a rich life.

August 9, 2000

> Today my doctor reviewed my treatment history. Daughters Karen and Susan joined me for the appointment. They asked relevant questions. The doctor is concerned about my high CAE count, which is supposed to measure cancer probability, and he wants to follow up with some additional blood tests and scans. As we walked to the car, we shared what we thought we heard. Each expressed appreciation for the doctor's frank analysis and response. In one of the silent moments the daughters turned toward me and said, "You know, Dad, we are all for you" and sealed the words with warm hugs. I managed to say, "I am all for you too." It was a grace-filled moment.

The fabric of my life is made up of various strands – my faith, the experiences that have come my way, my responses, and my beliefs and commitments. I am the product of those who have loved me and those I have loved. Into this fabric comes God's amazing, unrationed and healing grace to comfort, confront, renew and restore my soul and to take me through the sunny and cloudy days, the smooth and rough places and life's mountains and valleys. Thanks be to God for the gift of Jesus and his redemptive and reconciling life, call and compassionate spirit. For me reducing violence and increasing peace and justice have been my life passion! The journey has been interesting demanding, enriching, frustrating and deeply satisfying.

Each of you is on your own unique journey. You are at different places and travelling at different speeds and in different directions. Each reader has a special and valued configuration of gifts that both church and world desperately need. You also face exciting opportunities and challenges. My prayer for each one of you is that you will find a cause in which you can lose yourself and find deep joy in serving God and the human family.

Winifred and I, renewed our commitment to peace in the following millenium greeting:

> *We reaffirm our vocation is to praise and serve God; share God's transforming grace; keep hope alive; invite people to become reconciled to God, to each other and to themselves; to share God's freeing nonviolent alternative that transforms enemies into friends. This requires us to personally face, own, and deal with our own violence and to respond in reconciling love to the world's pain, brokeness, violence and war. This calls us to work for Shalom: justice, peace, health, well-being and wholeness for all people.*
>
> *We seek to follow the Jesus way of peacemaking until we are called home. We want to do this not with self-righteous piety, or a distorted sense of duty, but with love, humility, joy, hope, humor, and grace-filled hearts. We invite you to join us in responding to this continuing challenge.*

We Wish You a Reflective, Joyful, Blessed Millennium. . . .

> *Let us relax and rejoice*
> *in the coming of God's Son,*
> *and in God's unlimited love*
> *and unrationed Grace*
> *that calls us into Christ's ministry of*
> *reconciliation and healing.*

Peace, Joy, Hope and Love

Shalom is rooted in God's agape love and healing grace and seeks peace, justice, health, well-being and wholeness for God's creation, including all people on this planet. May Shalom penetrate and transform all who work for peace and justice, including the emerging Mennonite Church, into God's new community where "peace and justice embrace."

A Prayer for Shalom

God, each day may my faith generate shalom:
Let my dreams image shalom,
Let my mind think shalom,
Let my heart ignite shalom
Let my words invite shalom,
Let my deeds reflect shalom,
God, may your shalom transform my soul.

"There are three things that will endure—faith, hope, and love—and the greatest of these is love."

—I Corinthians 13

Selected Publications

"The Fight for Peace," *Christian Monitor*, January, 1933.

A Conceptual Framework for Guidance, Ph.D. Dissertation, The Ohio State University, 1958.

"A Conceptual Framework for Counseling with Particular Reference to the Concept of Adjustment," Proceedings of the 1959 Conference on Mennonite Educational and Cultural Problems.

"The Role of the Mennonite College in Education for World Mission," Proceedings of 1963 Conference on Mennonite Educational and Cultural Problems.

"Mississippi Diary," *Mennonite Weekly Review*, November 26, 1964.

""Report from Vietnam," *The Saturday Review*, Guest Editorial, December 3, 1966.

"Vietnam: Who Cares," (co-authored with Winifred Beechy), Herald Press: Scottdale, Pa., 1968.

"Peacemaking in Vietnam," *Peacemakers in a Broken World*. Editor, John A. Lapp, Herald Press: Scottdale, Pa., 1969.

After High School—What? The Herald Press: Scottdale, Pa., 1969.

The Church, The Reconciling Community (with Leader's Guide). Co-author of three chapters. Herald Press: Scottdale, Pa., 1970.

"India and the Changing Image of the U.S. in the Subcontinent." *Gospel Herald*, January 30, 1973.

"To Know and Understand," *Poland*, March 1975.

"The Civilian Public Service Experience," *Gospel Herald*, December 9, 1975.

"Psychological Factors in Female-Male Relationships," in *Which Way Women*, Editor, Dorothy Yoder Nyce, Mennonite Central Committee: Akron, Pa., 1980.

Space Theory of Personality: A Psychosocial Approach. Monograph, 1973. Revised 1975, 1976.

Counseling and Human Development: A Workbook for Beginning Students in Counseling, Monograph, 1979.

"What Mennonites Believe About the Military." Pamphlet, Mennonite Publishing House, 1980.

"Imprint on the World," *Goshen College Bulletin*, November 1984.

"China Educational Exchange," a paper read at a conference of the Indiana Consortium for International Programs, Goshen College, April 4, 1986.

"The Peacemaking Role of the Mennonite Central Committee," Pamphlet published by the Mennonite Central Committee: Akron, Pa., 1986.

"Psychology and Faith: Reflections of an Anabaptist," *Newsletter*, Mennonite Psychologists, Spring 1986.

"Psychological Factors in War and Peace," in Proceedings of the Conference on Higher Education and the Promotion of Peace, Bangkok, Thailand, December 1-3, 1986.

"Psychological Warfare," *Mennonite Weekly Review*, October 11, 1990. Also appeared in the Archbold (Ohio) *Buckeye* and the Wooster (Ohio) *Daily Record*.

"First They Make Enemies," Mennonite Central Committee Peace Office *Newsletter*, April 1991. Reprinted in Lutheran peace publication.

"Reflections on the Gulf War," *Goshen College Bulletin*, June 1991.

"Reflections of a Recycled Counselor," a paper read at the Association of Mennonite Psychologist's meeting, Pacific College, Fresno, Calif., March 1994.

"What Makes Atlee Run: My Faith Journey," Goshen College Chapel, May 3, 1994.

"Hewn Stones of Hope: A Personal Reflection on Martin Luther King," *Christian Living*, Winter, 1996.

"Reflections on Our Fifteen Years Together," *China Educational Exchange Update*, Fall, 1996.

"Raising Nonsexist Children" in *Women and Men, Gender in the Church*. Editor, Carol Penner, Herald Press: Scottdale, Pa., 1998.

"Service and Community," *Mennonite Life*. March 1999.

Compiled
April, 2000

Obituary of Atlee Beechy, 1914-2000

Atlee Beechy, professor emeritus of psychology and peace studies at Goshen College died at Goshen General Hospital Sunday, December 31, 2000, after an extended illness.

Beechy was born in Berlin, Ohio, on October 27, 1914, to Katie and George Beechy. He was married to Winifred Nelson May 24, 1941, in Goshen. She survives with three daughters: Karen Kreider of Royersford, Pa., Judy Beechy of Goshen and Susan Enz of Bordentown, N.J.; and six grandchildren.

Beechy's professional career included teaching at Goshen College and service with Mennonite Central Committee, Civilian Public Service, Vietnam Christian Service and China Educational Exchange. He traveled to many areas of need around the world, not just preaching peace, but working to create it.

Goshen College president Shirley H. Showalter said both Beechy and his wife Winifred have been mentors, friends and teachers for the college and world community.

Beechy, said Showalter, "spread 'unrationed grace' the way Johnny Appleseed spread apples. He was a stellar example of both the local and the cosmopolitan peacemaker – firmly rooted in Mennonite and Goshen College soil, and yet he was constantly praying for and concerned about those who suffered in other places around the world. In that, he is an example of the very highest aspirations of the GC motto, 'Culture for Service.'"

Beechy's staunch determination to work for peace was evident even in his youth. In a 1932 essay composed for Goshen College professor John Umble, later printed in the *Christian Monitor*, the 18-year-old Beechy wrote, "Christian churches must be an example and carry out the principles which the Prince of Peace has left for us to follow. The churches of every nation must teach their people that war is crime, the utter denial of the principles for which they stand."

Beechy began serving soon after he graduated from Goshen College in 1935 and earned a master's degree in education from Ohio State University in 1940. He taught in a one-room schoolhouse in Holmes County, Ohio, and later in the Columbus, Ohio, public school system. From 1943 to 1946 he and Winifred participated in Civilian Public Service assignments in Pennsylvania and South Dakota.

Following World War II, Beechy served as European director of the MCC Relief and Refugee program before returning to Goshen College in 1949. During his educational career, Beechy was dean of students, director of counseling services and professor of education, psychology and peace studies, helping found the college's peace program. In 1958 he received a doctorate in counseling psychology from Ohio State University.

J. Lawrence Burkholder, Goshen College president emeritus, reflected on Beechy's life in an interview with *The Elkhart Truth*: "He was interested in helping students rather than 'throwing the book' at them. I think he was a very fine educator, counselor and teacher, but he placed everything in an international perspective. . . . He at least did not flinch or give up in the face of all the problems we have in this world."

Beechy's focus on the world included a long association with MCC, including serving on its executive committee from

1961 to 1982. Beechy traveled to Africa, Asia, Europe, Central America and the Middle East on short-term MCC assignments. In 1966 Beechy directed Vietnam Christian Service, an inter-Protestant relief and refugee program. He and Winifred later wrote *Vietnam: Who Cares?*, published by Herald Press of Scottdale, Pa., about their experiences in that Asian country.

John Lapp, executive secretary of Mennonite Central Committee emeritus and former Goshen College dean and provost, said Beechy was an encourager of others, passionate for peace and remarkable for his half-century of overlapping work at Goshen College and MCC.

Lapp said, "I don't think it's possible to talk about the history of either institution from the '40s on without in some way touching Atlee. And it's hard to talk about Atlee without talking about Winifred."

Lapp continued, "Atlee was the maker of a circle of friends because he was *the* friend. He was a profoundly religious, Christian person, deeply devoted to the Christian way, the Sermon on the Mount. He oozed the oil of human kindness and divine love wherever he was, where they were."

The Beechys led Goshen College students in the first Study-Service Term programs in Poland in 1974 and China in 1980. That China experience led Beechy to help create China Educational Exchange, which he directed in 1981-82 and for which he continued as a program consultant through 1999.

Earlier in his career, Beechy was a Fulbright lecturer at the University of Allahabad in India and a consultant at Satya Wacuna University in Indonesia during sabbatical leaves from the college.

In 1987 Beechy co-founded Seniors for Peace, a Goshen-based group which works to harness the skills and energies of retirees and senior citizens to work for peace. A decade later, the Beechys received the Mennonite Church's first "Keep the

Faith, Share the Peace" recognition created to recognize people who have lived for peace.

Clair Hochstetler, Goshen General Hospital chaplain, was with the Beechy family during Atlee Beechy's last days. Beechy's devout Christian witness continued to the end, Hochstetler said, as he sang and worshiped with family members and offered a personal blessing to each of them the day before his death.

"Atlee showed us all how to live with grace, dignity and a passion for peace – and he is now . . . a model for dying well, just as he lived," said Hochstetler.

Beechy was a member of College Mennonite Church where a memorial service was held January 5, 2001.

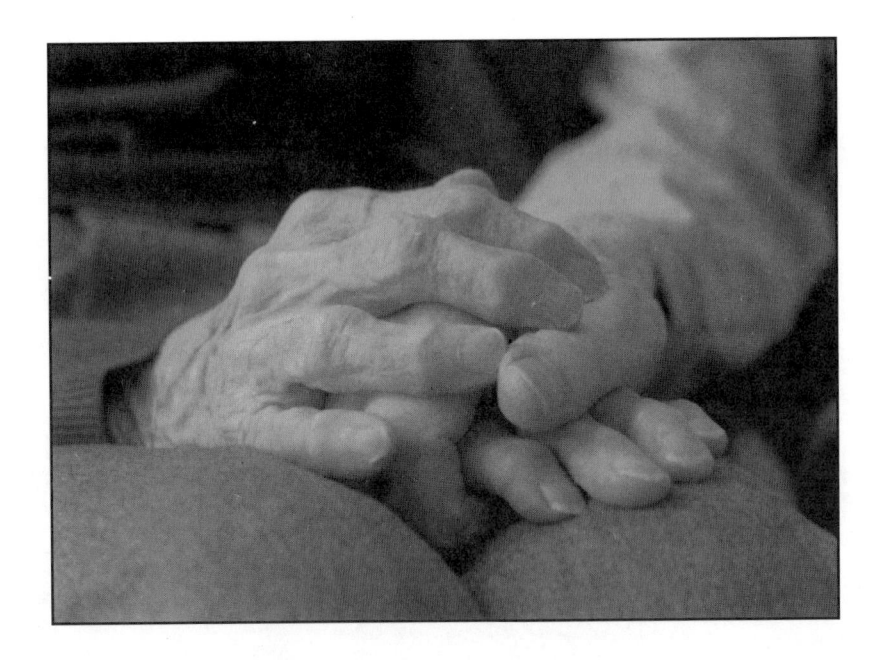